FOREW

The aim of this book is to provide you with guidance, support, structure and encouragement to enable you to deliver successful presentations. Irrespective of whether you are new to presenting or seeking to refine your existing knowledge and experience gathered over many years, this book seeks to give everyone something new to learn.

The principles advocated in this book apply to presentations whether they are to be delivered to colleagues in your organisation or from outside of it and, unless specifically mentioned within the text, apply to audiences both large and small.

The possible range of topics that could be the basis of a presentation is endless, a few are used to illustrate some of the advocated techniques. Whenever there are alternatives from which a choice can be made, choose the one best suited to your particular topic.

One final note, we would recommend initially reading the book from cover to cover, since some of the content in later chapters is reliant on having an understanding of the earlier ones.

Thank you, enjoy the read and, perhaps more importantly, find out how to really enjoy making successful presentations.

CHAPTER 1

Setting a goal for your presentation

Where do you start? You've just been given the topic of a presentation and that's it, you know nothing more. It's not a lot of help really. You could end up delivering a presentation that your audience is not interested in, that doesn't deliver what your boss wanted and is a personal nightmare. To avoid these disasters, we'll show you the importance of asking questions, lots of questions, so you can develop a presentation that interests your audience, delivers success for your organisation and gives you a really positive feeling.

So that's where we will start: chapter 1 is about determining the aim of your presentation so you are set up for success irrespective of whether your audience is large or small, drawn from within your organisation or elsewhere.

DIFFERENT TYPES OF PRESENTATIONS

There are three basic presentation types:

Type 1: **To give information**

Here, you need to pass specific knowledge to your audience which they do not already have. So you'll probably be tempted to do all the talking, but as we will see later, if only you talk, there will be no guarantee that the audience understands the message (assuming, that is, they stay awake!).

Type 2: **To facilitate a discussion.**

Well this sounds a little better than the one above, at least we are hoping for some form of 'discussion' during your presentation. A few more people might stay awake (especially those who like to talk, we'll learn how to deal with those people later). Alas, the danger here is that discussions are often inconclusive with no real outcome.

Type 3: **To stimulate action.**

The purpose of your presentation could be, for instance, to tell staff to adopt new working practices, although *persuading* (rather than *telling*) would deliver better long-term results. Maybe you want someone to buy your company's products or perhaps you just want the audience to enjoy a good laugh! These presentations are all designed to achieve some form of reaction.

You can see above that the first two types have their challenges, and we will look later at how these can be overcome. But if you are looking for an early hint as to what makes a presentation 'great' rather than 'okay', look no further than adopting the third type, to stimulate action.

> Great presentations provoke a reaction in the audience and encourage them to take action.

Let's practise what we have so far:

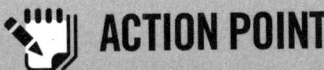 **ACTION POINT**

Think of a topic for a presentation. We're going to develop your idea throughout the chapter, so if you can think of one that you have to give in the next few weeks or months, so much the better. Any subject will do, it could be work-related or simply a speech you have to give at a wedding. You choose.

So which type of presentation is it going to be? To give information, facilitate a discussion or stimulate action?

PRIMARY AND PERSONAL AIMS

There are two aims you need to set yourself: a primary and a personal aim.

What's the difference? A primary aim is about your presentation being a success and the personal aim is about you achieving success as presenter. Let's look at an example:

ℚ EXAMPLE

As Sales Manager for a toy importer, Ian was asked by his boss to deliver a presentation on their products. Ian needed to develop his brief (by asking questions) into a primary aim that would enable him, having delivered the presentation, to know that it had been successful. He also needed to define what would make him a successful presenter on this occasion – perhaps he wanted a standing ovation when he finished – and that would be defined in his personal aim.

Why separate the two aims? Well, it's one thing to tell your audience that your aim is to convince them to buy your products, but I don't think they would like to be told that Ian expected a standing ovation! So there's a personal, unpublished aim for the presenter and a primary, published aim for the presentation itself.

We will now concentrate on the primary aim and will return later to developing your personal, secondary aim when we look at your nerves, your stress level or your sheer enjoyment (yes, it's more than possible!) when you make a presentation.

Developing your primary aim

We need to refine your type of message into a primary aim by asking some questions. Here are the first three:

1. What am I seeking to achieve?
2. Why is this presentation being made?
3. How would I recognise success?

Staying with Ian's example above, here's how he might have answered these questions:

1. *What am I seeking to achieve?* To encourage existing customers to buy a wider range of products.
2. *Why is this presentation being made?* Because sales targets are being missed.
3. *How would I recognise success?* There will be a 5% increase in the next quarter's sales figures.

These answers would have encouraged Ian to deliver an upbeat selling pitch, offering full praise of all the available products and perhaps offering bulk-buying discounts.

Asking yourself these questions, as the presenter, is one way of defining the aim, but you might get very different answers if you ask the same questions of the person(s) requesting you to make the presentation. Let's look at the summarised answers given by Ian's boss to the same questions:

1. *What am I seeking to achieve?* To counter press reports that the company's imported toys are unsafe and, as a result, should be removed from sale.
2. *Why is this presentation being made?* To take back the initiative and stall the possible company bankruptcy that could result.

3. *How would I recognise success?* To halt the sales decline, secure a
   right of reply in the national press and avoid bankruptcy.

In the examples above, we would have two very different
presentations, in style and in content, even though they both
address the initial brief to talk about the company's products.
Imagine how Ian would have felt if he had tried to deliver his
upbeat presentation when, in reality, the audience just wanted to
harangue the company about their disregard for public safety?

> You must refine any answers until you have total clarity of what
> the primary aim of the presentation is and how the presentation
> would be judged a success.

 ACTION POINT

Ask the three key questions of your chosen topic:

1   What am I seeking to achieve?
2   Why is this presentation being made?
3   How would I recognise success?

Keep asking these questions until you have precise answers.

Defining your primary aim

You can now bring your answers together to define your primary
aim. This will accurately summarise what you are trying to achieve
and the ways that you will be able to measure success. Let's look
at Ian's situation again to illustrate:

Ian's primary aim was: to convince the national press to take
action in support of the company by persuading the buying public
that their toys are safe. Success will be measured by:

1. An immediate stop to further negative press comment.
2. Securing an opportunity for a 'right of reply' which will be
   printed in the press in the next relevant editions.
3. Slowing the decline in sales to half its current rate of collapse
   within the next week through positive press intervention.

4. Avoiding corporate bankruptcy as a consequence of the poor press coverage.

5. The presentation lasting no more than one hour.

Measuring success

In the example above, there are five different ways that we could judge success. Why not keep it simple and have just the one? With one measure of success, if you fail to achieve it, even by the smallest fraction, your presentation would be judged a failure. And a failed presentation is not part of the remit of this book! Yet if you fail to meet just one of five measures, you can still rightly claim to have given a presentation which is 80% successful.

So when defining your primary aim, think of as many measures as you can that would deem the presentation successful. One more point about measuring success:

> Even when you think that you have delivered a superb presentation, if your audience has not understood, you will have failed totally.

For example you could speak in the most eloquent French but if your audience doesn't understand French, it will fail completely! So all presentations must include some form of checking that you have created **understanding**.

Timing your presentation

How long have you been given for your presentation? One of your measures of success should be that you have kept to the allotted time, although if you have achieved your aim and have five minutes to spare, never waffle to fill in the time. The rule is to 'quit whilst you are ahead', (unless another presenter is following on from you and they are not ready to take over).

> A good presentation finishes on time, but it is better to finish a little early than to talk just to fill the space.

Multiple primary aims

There may be occasions when you want to achieve more than just one of the three *types* of presentations in one session. Sometimes this will be relatively straightforward:

Q EXAMPLE

In Ian's presentation, he needed to give out information before he could persuade the press to take action; this means that the former purpose (information giving, type one) is then set aside in favour of the latter (persuading, type three).

However, combining more than one type of primary aim can be troublesome. If Ian decided that it was right for him to *discuss* product safety with the press, it would have become a session where accusations and possibly insults would be traded. Having created such an atmosphere, it would have been incredibly difficult for him to then conclude with a press commitment to a positive course of action. So whilst Ian didn't intend to ban press participation in the presentation, he would need to manage it very tightly throughout.

Now let's consolidate where you are up to in this chapter by continuing with the exercise:

 ACTION POINT

Taking your earlier work, define your primary aim. Make sure it has multiple measures by which success can be judged.

Five tests of your primary aim

Much as you might want to rush in and start writing your presentation at this point, we need to test your primary aim before proceeding further.

> How to test your primary aim for validity:
> Test 1: Is it agreed with the person(s) requesting the presentation?
> Test 2: Is it reasonable to expect success?
> Test 3: Is a presentation the right medium for this aim?
> Test 4: Will your audience perceive it as worthwhile?
> Test 5: Are you the right presenter?

Test 1: Is it agreed?

We have already demonstrated in our example the potential disaster if your primary aim does not match that defined by others. Your primary aim must meet the expectations of the person(s) who requested that you develop the presentation, whether they are your boss, your audience or a conference organiser.

Test 2: Is it reasonable?

This test has to be applied to both the overall aim and the individual measures for judging success. There could be a wide range of factors that contribute to 'reasonableness': can it be achieved within your allotted time? Will the people needed to achieve your aim be available? Is the aim just 'an impossible dream'? You will know or can discover all these factors, so make a judgment.

Test 3: Is it the right medium?

Having developed the primary aim, it may well be that a presentation is the wrong medium to achieve it. Perhaps you only need one person in the audience and a presentation would be formal overkill. Or maybe it is highly technical information that could be sent out via an email or a written report. Decide whether or not a presentation is the right medium to achieve your primary aim.

Test 4: Will it be worthwhile?

Will the audience consider it a good use of their time? The audience must believe before, during and after your presentation that it has been worthwhile. If you expect 10 people to travel

100 miles for your 15 minute presentation, it will have to be a very special presentation to make them believe it was worth their while. (You could improve their perspective if you eliminated the need for them to travel, perhaps by travelling to them instead.)

Test 5: Are you the right person?
You don't have to be the world's expert on a subject to present it, although knowing a *little* more than members of the audience will always help! So don't discount yourself too quickly.

Broadly, when looking at the three types of presentations:
- If you are giving information, you *must* know more than the audience, if only to answer their questions.
- If the presentation is to stimulate a discussion, you do *not need* to know more about the subject than the audience, but you *do need* to know how to facilitate discussions.
- If the presentation is to stimulate action, you do *not need* to know more than your audience, but you may need to be in a position of authority or expertise to succeed.

Has your primary aim passed all the tests?

Obviously, if your primary aim passes all five tests, you can move on to preparing your presentation. Failing any one (or more) of the tests should cause you to re-think the whole idea of making such a presentation. However, do remember that a presentation is a highly effective way to persuade, influence and, on a more personal note, raise your profile. So it is worth trying to make a presentation work.

 **ACTION POINT**

Ask yourself the following question: Does your primary aim pass the five tests?
If the answer is yes, you can start to develop your presentation.
If the answer is no, what have you learnt about how your original goal can and should be achieved?

🔍 EXAMPLE

So how did these tests apply to our example? Applying these five tests meant that everything changed for Ian's presentation:

- **Test 1: Is it agreed?**: *Pass (once his boss's answers were incorporated).*
- **Test 2: Is it reasonable?**: *Fail. The measures were unachievable within the allotted time.*
- **Test 3: Is this the right medium?**: *Fail. To succeed, a whole series of other activities were needed rather than just a presentation. For example: one-to-one meetings with the press, reports from respected and independent agencies).*
- **Test 4: Is it worthwhile?**: *Fail. Ian would not be able to convince the press that it was worthwhile attending.*
- **Test 5: Is Ian the right presenter?**: *Fail. The last person asked to undertake such a primary aim should be the Sales Manager since his motivation would immediately be challenged by the press.*

The testing of Ian's primary aim could have been stopped after the first failure, but applying the last three tests gave valuable learning points. The idea of a presentation was therefore abandoned and instead a company 'rescue' plan was developed.

You may be asking why I have used Ian's example in this chapter, which concluded that a presentation would have been the wrong course of action. After all, isn't this book supposed to be trying to convince you that presentations are an invaluable tool and can be immensely satisfying to the presenter and audience alike? Absolutely! Presentations *are* invaluable and they *will* be immensely satisfying by the time you finish reading this book. However, you should also use this book to make sure you don't wander into a situation which is inherently a mistake. This book's goal is to set you up to succeed in your presenting, not drift into failure.

Stay focused. Your primary aim is your map, your steering wheel and your destination for all your preparation and delivery. Use it.

TOP TIPS

QUICK RECAP

- *Define the primary aim of your presentation: what is your presentation seeking to achieve?*
- *Identify multiple ways to measure the success of a presentation.*
- *There are three main types of presentations: to give information, facilitate a discussion or stimulate action.*
- *Ensure that you will know at the end of a presentation that the audience have understood what you intended to convey. Understanding is one of the main measures of success for a presentation.*
- *Apply the five tests to your presentation's primary aim to determine whether or not it is: agreed by others; realistic in its ambition; the right medium; worthwhile; and to be delivered by the right person, you!*
- *Use your primary aim to focus your attention during the preparation and delivery of your presentation.*

CHAPTER 2

Researching and sifting content

Have you ever been to a presentation and been overwhelmed with information? A presentation so packed with information that you couldn't remember any of it? Or maybe the presenter started by giving a 30 page handout and asked what you thought about the content?

Information overload is like pressing the self-destruct button for any presentation. So is the secret to say the least amount possible? Not exactly. You need the *right* amount of information to achieve your primary aim *and* you also need enough further information to answer at least the majority of related questions – it's a fine balancing act (one of many you will need for success). So this chapter is about conducting your research and getting the information balance right.

YOUR EXISTING KNOWLEDGE

> Just because you think you know everything that needs to be said in a presentation, don't assume that there wouldn't be benefit in undertaking research.

You know lots of things. Maybe you know lots of things about the topic for your forthcoming presentation. Great. Sometimes, however, our memories are not quite as good as we might like. For example: do you remember how much you last paid for a pint of milk – without checking the receipt? This section is about not just what we know but also what we *think* we know and we need to bear this in mind when we start our research. A good starting point is to forget about anything you know or *think* you know.

Now this might sound a little weird – and perhaps it is. Let's say I am going to make a presentation to you about how to confidently present to audiences of over a thousand people. There are a myriad of other people's experiences that I can draw on, but if I concentrate on just one of my experiences, the whole presentation would narrow in its remit.

Q EXAMPLE

I was once asked to interrupt a retiring Managing Director making his farewell speech with a personal life story, introducing friends, family and colleagues from his present and past. Concentrating on that experience, will prompt me to remember how difficult it was to say the word 'peculiarity', how my knees bounced up and down like jack-hammers and how I managed an audience that had spent the last few hours drinking copious amounts of wine.

Yet there is so much more that I should say to achieve my aim, by drawing on a wider range of experiences than my own, so it is better to put aside your own experiences, at least for now. (Just in case you are wondering, my solutions to the challenges above were: to script the word 'peculiarity' as it sounds (using phonetics), to wear very baggy trousers to disguise my bouncing knee-caps and enjoy the event *with* the merry audience rather than seeking to manage or fight them.)

Bearing all this in mind then, it is obvious that to make any presentation a success you will need to conduct research to add to your existing knowledge and experiences, even if you are already an expert on your topic.

RESEARCHING NEW INFORMATION

Sources for your research

So where can you look for information to achieve your primary aim? Here are a few possible sources:

- Books, publications, the internet, libraries
- Professional bodies, (other) experts
- Organisations or colleagues who might have relevant experiences, skills or related documents
- Corporate and management information
- The audience themselves (find out examples from them in advance to illustrate your presentation)

Once you have gathered all your research, add it to what you know and what you think you know.

Conflicting information

Successful research will frequently identify conflicting inform-ation. One piece of research might say 'the colour red looks good on walls, it is seductive, passionate'. Another source might say that 'red can stimulate anger and aggression'. Yet another, that 'people can't stay in rooms painted red for long'. So which piece of information is right? Which are you going to gather? The simple answer is: all of it!

Contradictory information is a bonus; it will prompt you to draw your own independent conclusions. A good researcher will be open to all available information.

Copyright information

Just because you have found information, do not assume you can use it.

There might be copyright restrictions and you must check these out and perhaps seek necessary permissions before deciding whether or not to include it.

Organising your research

You will need to access your research easily when you start developing your presentation. Perhaps you can organise it in a computer file, or even an in- tray or a desk drawer. It really doesn't matter, but you must organise it. You could:

• List the various sources and, as you develop your presentation, look up each reference in turn.

• Copy out everything you discover (remembering the rules of copyright), ideally under key headings.

• Note key words or phrases to prompt you.

Find the way that suits you best. One method I recommend is to:

• Place the primary aim in front of you.

• Note everything under a series of headings, which develop as you gather more information (because you won't think of all possible headings at the start).

• Rather than copy/type large amounts of information from one source, simply note a reference (perhaps a book title and page numbers) under the appropriate heading.

Make sure you find a system that works for you, as you need to be able to easily find the information when preparing your presentation.

Whilst undertaking your research, avoid judging whether or not you agree with it. You must suspend your judgment at this time to avoid the danger of only paying attention to that which you want to hear.

Fact or ...?

It can be useful at this point to classify your research into that which is factual and that which is not, perhaps thoughts, opinions, beliefs or feelings. Why? Because if you are going to make a persuasive presentation, one in which you intend to stimulate action, facts are invaluable in handling potential audience resistance.

Q EXAMPLE

A politician says 'I think that we should go to war against another country.' Many people would question whether or not it was the right thing to do because it is solely based on what someone else thinks. Yet if the same politician based their conclusions on factual events, events which therefore cannot be disputed, and stated that the inevitable conclusion from those facts was to declare war, many more people might be inclined to support the war.

Your research should be classified according to the quality of the information, its status if you like, and one way to do this is to work through the following classifications:

FACTOR:

F: Facts: an indisputable piece of information.

A: Absolutes: rules, regulations, instructions and the law

C: Conclusions/judgments: based on the facts or absolutes

T: Tenets/beliefs: of a group or society

O: Opinions and thoughts: from respected sources

R: Reactions: generated by people's senses, feelings or passions

🔍 EXAMPLE

Let's see how our politician could have made a more persuasive speech to solicit support for a war:

'Our neighbour's military has crossed our borders [VF] and killed over 100 citizens [VF]. The invasion of our country and the killing of our citizens is a breach of international law [A] and we have both the right [A] and responsibility [C] to seek redress and defend ourselves. It is a violation of our basic freedoms that are encoded into our everyday lives [T] and we must therefore take action [C] to defend our people and our country with all of our strength and courage when faced with such aggression [R].'

As we can see the politician has progressed through the FACTOR classifications to create a far more persuasive argument for war. Because of this, he is far more likely to get the results he wants.

Note: VF means that it has been verified from more than one source

USING YOUR RESEARCH

Consider putting your research aside

This is the second time I have asked you to put information to one side. So how does this work?

Whilst writing this book on making *Successful Presentations*, having familiarised myself with my research, I put it to one side to bring my own thought processes to bear and create the best work that I can devise for you, the reader. Naturally, if I needed a key reference or got stuck, I used my research.

There are occasions, however, when you must stick closely to your research and the information you have.

Q EXAMPLE

In the global stock-market crash of 2008, one wrong word by people in key financial roles could have worsened what was an already disastrous situation. So meetings took place to co-ordinate the response of governments around the world. In such situations, sticking to a 'script' was essential to try to secure financial stability.

However, a cautionary note here:

Avoid, whenever possible, using someone else's script verbatim for a presentation – even if you have to express their views.

Q EXAMPLE

I remember a time at school when I had to make a presentation to my class. I was supposed to have written it the previous evening as part of my homework, but persuaded my dad to write it for me. He was an accomplished public speaker so I thought I could get higher marks if I used the skills available to me at home! I even copied it into my own handwriting to complete the deception. Alas, my teacher was not convinced that it was my homework and asked me to explain a term I had used, 'a telescopic bar'. I had no idea! Whilst I still believe that my punishment exceeded the crime, it did teach me a key lesson – never use someone else's script! (For the record, a telescopic bar is a brass rail that could be drawn across a corridor like a telescope to bar entry and retracted to give admittance.)

Categorising your research

Next, categorise your research into three groups:

What **must** you communicate?

These pieces of information will be the absolute minimum that must be communicated to achieve your primary aim. It will be a short list, perhaps a 15 minute presentation will contain no more than three or four such points. If the audience remembers these few points and nothing more, the primary aim will still have been achieved (but only just).

What **should** you communicate?

As presenters, we actually want to achieve more than the basic minimum. So this question expands the information given above to enhance the quality, efficiency and effectiveness by which our success will be measured. If the audience remembers this information as well as the essentials mentioned above, we would excel in achieving our primary aim.

What **could** you communicate?

This is non-essential information related to your primary aim. If the audience does not remember this information, you will still have achieved total success of your primary aim. This will frequently include relevant jokes, anecdotes or different perspectives on how a similar outcome could be achieved. For example if you are making a presentation on how to self-complete a tax return, you could suggest that they hire an accountant to do it for them!

Leave some research out

TOP TIPS

Only retain the information from your research that **must**, **should** or **could** be communicated to achieve your primary aim. Discard the rest.

You might reasonably argue that, if you have truly focused on your primary aim, you would only have collated research that must, should or could be communicated. However, the danger in categorising information as you research, is that you might ignore something that will be useful later.

Take the example I quoted earlier on red-painted walls. Even if my presentation is just about the colour red, I might still need to know which colours might also prompt similar responses. So my research needs to be somewhat broader than my primary aim.

 **ACTION POINT**

Write the following primary aim at the top of a blank sheet of paper:
By the end of this presentation, each member of the audience will know how to wash the pots.
Then divide the page into three rows, labelling each 'must say', 'should say' and 'could say' in that order and fill in your answers. (It is okay for this example to rely solely on your existing knowledge of the subject).
When you have completed the exercise, compare your answers with those reproduced towards the end of this chapter.

Validating your content

When you have categorised your research, you must validate your work to date. Check:

1. If you only communicate what you **must** say, would you successfully achieve your primary aim? In the exercise, would the audience have learned how to wash pots?
2. Have you made any assumptions that need to be verified or explained? For example in the above exercise, have you assumed that the audience has access to water? Possesses pots? Has a degree of physical dexterity? *Assumptions are dangerous, beware!*
3. Will your audience be *guaranteed to* understand any terminology/language you have used? (We will return to this in more detail when we look at the role of the audience in delivering successful presentations.)
4. In reviewing the content against your research, has anything been missed, invented or misrepresented?

5. Have you adhered to copyright laws?

6. If you have been given a specified period of time for your presentation, will that be enough time to at least say that which you must? If not, you will need to either secure a longer time-frame or reduce the scope of your primary aim. And if you have now changed the content in any way, ask again:

7. If you only communicate what you must say, would you successfully achieve your primary aim?

How these categories of what *must*, *should* and *could* be communicated are used

We will be returning to these categories throughout this book. To give you an idea of their importance, we will need them to:

• Develop your script
• Create visual aids
• Help your audience keep track of your presentation
• Project your voice
• Choreograph your body language
• Adjust your script during your presentation if, for any reason, you either have too much or too little time remaining
• Prepare answers to questions from the audience

So if you haven't yet completed the exercise above, do it now!

Now compare your answer from Action Point on p.23 to to that produced below. Please note: it doesn't matter if you don't totally agree with my example.

Primary Aim: By the end of this presentation, each member of the audience will know how to wash the pots.

What **must** you communicate to achieve your primary aim?
1. Get some pots.
2. Get some clean water.
3. Create an interaction between the clean water and the pots to cleanse the latter with the former.

By acting on these three points, the pots should be cleaner, but not necessarily hygienically spotless – whilst that degree of cleanliness is what **should** be achieved, it is not necessarily what **must** be achieved.

What **should** you communicate to excel in achieving your primary aim?
1. Use soap and hot (but not scalding) water to enhance the end result.
2. Ensure your hands are clean before starting.
3. The water should be either in a clean bowl or from a running tap.
4. Use an aid to cleaning, for example a scourer.
5. Having washed the pots, inspect them for cleanliness.
6. Place the cleansed pots onto a clean surface to ensure your effort is not wasted.

Note: You may have placed some of this information in the **must** box above. If so, ask yourself whether or not it is absolutely essential to fulfil the primary aim as defined.

What non-essential information **could** you communicate?
1. You could personally avoid the task by getting someone else to do it.
2. If you only used disposable pots, you don't need to listen to this presentation.
3. Buy a dishwasher instead.
4. One idea might be to use clean sand rather than water.

Let's now apply this to a more relevant example:

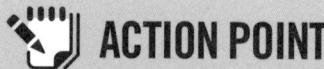 **ACTION POINT**

1 Define a primary aim for a presentation you have to make (or invent one).
2 Plan how you will organise your research.
3 Conduct your research.
4 Add to your research what you already know (or think) you know about the topic.
5 Classify your research using FACTOR.
6 Using your primary aim, determine what **must**, **should** and **could** be communicated.
7 Validate (using the checklist above) that you will achieve your primary aim.

QUICK RECAP

- *A balance must be achieved to ensure you give the right amount of information for your audience to absorb and still achieve your primary aim.*
- *Before you start researching, determine how you will organise the information you gather.*
- *When embarking on research, forget everything that you think you know about the subject.*
- *Good research will find contradicting information. This is healthy, it helps you to make up your own mind up about issues.*
- *The information you gather during your research may well be subject to copyright restrictions. Make sure you check.*
- *Seek out as many possible sources of information as possible.*
- *When you have investigated all other sources of information, add your own knowledge and experience.*
- *Classifying information into different types (eg facts) will help to ensure that you will use the information to the best effect.*
- *Once you have become familiar with the research, consider putting it to one side whilst you develop your presentation.*
- *Categorise the information into what you **must**, **should** and **could** communicate to achieve your primary aim.*
- *Before signing off on the work you have undertaken, validate that you have adhered to the principles contained in this chapter and that the presentation will achieve your primary aim.*

CHAPTER 3

Your audience

Imagine your reaction if you bought theatre tickets to watch Shakespeare's *Twelfth Night* and you ended up watching the musical *Les Miserables*? Imagine how you would feel if you had spent weeks developing a presentation and no-one turned up to listen? An audience can destroy your chance of achieving success if they turn up and hear something they didn't expect just as easily as if they didn't turn up at all. We need to get our audience 'on-side' to be successful – so how do we do that? This chapter takes you through the necessary steps to getting your audience on your side.

DECLARE YOUR PRIMARY AIM

In chapter one, I quoted an example of a mismatch between what the presenter intended (selling his products) and the audience (who just wanted to complain about the poor quality of those products). If ever there was a recipe for disaster, this was it! So publish your primary aim to ensure that the audience coming to your presentation has the same purpose in mind. Then, ask a sample of your invitees what they think your presentation is about – does their understanding of your primary aim match your own?

An additional step will be needed when others are sending out the invites to your presentation. Check the distributors' understanding of your primary aim before asking them to send it.

Either way, success will be dependent upon your presentation fulfilling the expectations of your audience.

Undeclared primary aims

It is perhaps appropriate at this stage to talk about primary aims that are not published in advance and what impact this can have on the audience. For example: you wouldn't pre-announce your intention to declare half the workforce redundant or forewarn people of a corporate takeover. So you cannot always publish the purpose of your presentation in advance, although that will not stop people speculating as to its purpose. To minimise speculation in this scenario:

- Give people the minimum amount of notice they will need to adjust their diaries (and so lessen the opportunity for gossip).
- Quash rumours of a destructive or overly-negative nature that are unrelated to your presentation (but avoid answering questions which effectively reveal the primary aim because it is the only issue left).
- Keep your intended audience as busy as possible on other issues before they arrive.

WHO TO INVITE

TOP TIPS

Don't just invite the people needed for you to succeed in your primary aim.

Invite potentially awkward people and those who support your aim.

If you follow this advice your audience will be made up of three possible groups: those needed to achieve your primary aim, those who have the power or influence to wreck any chance of success before or after your presentation, and those who have the power or influence to outweigh any challenges that might arise.

ACTION POINT

Let's continue planning for the primary aim you defined in the Action Point on p.26:

- Who must you invite to achieve success?
- Who might oppose your aim and should therefore be invited?
- Who can you invite to counter-balance any negativity?

Special needs

Now you know who you are going to invite, you must ensure that they are given every opportunity to get the most out of your presentation. You will need to ask if they have any special needs and, if necessary, how you might best accommodate them. For example, certain people may:

- Be unable to look at a projected image.
- Have difficulty assimilating the written word at the same speed as others.
- Be physically unable to access certain locations, with or without help.

- Be physically uncomfortable if expected to sit or stand in a given position for a period of time.
- Have impaired hearing or eyesight.
- Be unable to stay comfortably in a room which has no natural daylight.
- Need to go to the toilet more frequently than others.

> People with special needs are neither less worthy to receive your message nor less able to understand it – unless, that is, you fail to respond to those needs.

Invitations that work

Your invitees will want a number of questions answered before accepting your (or the organiser's) invitation. Let's start with the basics:

- What is the title and (primary) aim of the presentation?
- What, if anything, will I need to prepare or bring with me?
- Who is the presenter?
- Where should I go? This should not just be a room number! You might need to give location details, including how to get there. You could include a GPS reference, a map and public transport options (don't assume everyone has access to a car).
- When do I need to arrive by? This is different from when will the presentation start – it will provide time for people to find their seats, grab a drink or whatever.
- When can I expect to leave? People like to know the *latest* time that they will be free to take on other commitments or travel home.
- How will my special needs, if I have any, be accommodated?
- Do I need to confirm that I will attend and, if so, how?

However, you need an invitation to do more than just provide instruction. You must briefly explain to your audience why they are *needed*. (Use the word 'need' rather than 'want' – people are less inclined to question the former.) Specifying their essential role in helping you to achieve your primary aim should also ensure anyone deputised to stand in for them will be adequately briefed and have the necessary delegated authority to fulfil your requirements.

Picking up on an earlier theme in chapter one, you also need to make it *worthwhile* for them to attend: what will they get in return for giving you their time? This is often expressed as an acronym: WIIFM. [What's in it for me?]

TOP TIPS

Give people a WIIFM

WIIFMs can be negative or (preferably) positive – the latter says what they will gain by listening, the former what they might lose if they don't.

The audience will be motivated to attend for different reasons, so don't rely on just one WIIFM.

🔍 EXAMPLE

Let's look at how this might work for a forthcoming presentation I might make to independently owned booksellers:

Meet the author of Successful Presentations
on Friday, 4 January at the home of Crimson Publishing

The new Successful *range of books from Crimson Publishing is fast becoming a 'must-have' for everyone and the latest on Presentations is no exception. Brian Lomas, the author, will be presenting just a few of the highlights from an exciting new series and an informative read at 4pm on 4 January. He will also answer any questions you might have about presenting.*

Crimson's chief editor will also give the promotional launch details for the entire series, which is something you just cannot afford to miss! Less than two hours of your time could see your sales rocketing!

Places are limited, so please confirm quickly if you can come along to what we are sure will be an entertaining and rewarding afternoon.

A map and GPS location is attached. Should you have any access requirements (or other needs), please do let us know.

Let's look at the positive characteristics of this invitation in more detail:

- It is brief
- Jargon has been avoided (such as 'the primary aim')
- It includes different motivational reasons to attend:
  a. A personal WIIFM: Their personal presentation questions will be answered.
  b. A business WIIFM: The promise of rising sales without the hard-sell.
  c. A customer WIIFM: Stocking the range will satisfy customer demand.
- It creates a sense of urgency on a number of levels:
  a. Suggesting that they will miss out on sales unless they act quickly.
  b. Telling of a forthcoming promotional launch.
  c. Limiting the number of available places suggests they need to act quickly.
- 'Rewarding' seeks to consolidate all the above messages into one key, closing phrase

The above invite has been written for independent booksellers (the only invitees). However, if the presentation was also open to journalists who review books, I would write a second (and very different) invite to motivate their attendance.

Write as many different invitations as necessary to ensure everyone invited is motivated to attend your presentation.

TOP TIPS

 ACTION POINT

Using the attendance list you developed earlier, write invitations to motivate everyone on your list to attend.

WHAT YOU SHOULD KNOW ABOUT YOUR AUDIENCE

You've given information to your audience, now it is time they gave you some back. We have already started gathering some information by asking:

- What do you think we are seeking to achieve in the presentation?
- Will you be attending? (You need to know the size of your audience to plan the logistics).
- What, if any, special needs do you have? (This would include any special dietary requirements if you are providing refreshments).

And now we need to ask more: You should find out from your audience:

1. What do they already *know* about the subject to be presented? What terminology do you *know* they know?

Finding out more about the audience can only improve your presentation.

TOP TIPS

2. What is their initial *reaction* to the primary aim?
3. What can you learn about them to help build rapport?
4. What happened in the best presentations they have ever attended?

But be careful how this information is gathered, you don't want to cause offence before the presentation has even started!

What does the audience know – or think they know?

You will need to be discreet and perhaps indirect here to avoid suggesting that your audience has a lack of knowledge or understanding. Show your presentation (or part of it) to a few members of your intended audience and ask: 'How many of the *other* people in the audience will understand it?' This should give you an impression of the 'average' level of understanding.

> You should 'pitch' your presentation above the average level of understanding so that the majority will readily conclude that they have learnt from your presentation.
>
> But do not ignore those with greater or lesser knowledge.

For those who know the least about your subject, their difficulty will typically arise from being given too much information (and we discussed appropriate avoidance techniques in the last chapter), or their lack of understanding of acronyms, abbreviations or terminology.

Q EXAMPLE

During one company's induction, I found that the staff used acronyms almost as a second language. So I asked what each stood for – it seemed a perfectly reasonable thing for me to do. Alas, I caused considerable embarrassment when some of the most experienced people in the business didn't know the answer – and the longer they had worked there, the greater their reluctance to find out for themselves. Crazy but true and yet it is an easy thing to fix.

To avoid the pitfalls of assuming your audience understands acronyms, abbreviations or terminology:

- Show (without discussion) pre-prepared visual aids that explain any jargon. For instance: verbally we might say 'PC', but on a visual aid we would show 'PC (Political Correctness)'.
- Explain jargon with a smile. For instance: 'Just in case you were wondering if you are in the right presentation, the abbreviation PC in this presentation refers not to Personal Computers but rather Political Correctness.'
- Distribute a glossary of acronyms, abbreviations and terminology before you start speaking. It will only be read by those who need it.

Your goal should be to ensure that the person with the least knowledge has the opportunity to gain total understanding.

At the opposite end of the knowledge scale is the 'know-it-all'. We have all met someone who *always* know best, whose opinions *must* be heard and who believe they will learn *nothing* from anyone else. To convince them to attend, explain that they will have a special role to play – perhaps they could be asked to check you are delivering the right message, help you to answer difficult questions or give you feedback (after the event) on your presentation. It may be a few 'white-lies', but they will feel that you have shown them (and their knowledge) the respect that they *think* they deserve and it is likely to reduce the number and voracity of any interruptions they might be tempted to make.

What's the initial reaction of your audience?

You do not want your audience to make up their minds about your presentation before you give it, but people will form an opinion nonetheless. Think of a politician you love to hate. Every time he or she starts speaking on television, how do you react? Do you actually give them a fair hearing or do you just think they cannot be trusted before they even start? I suspect the latter, it is certainly a trap I fall into frequently. I trust that you won't create such a strong reaction with your would-be audience, but your primary aim might. It will be useful for you to know the preconceived ideas of at least a sample of the audience before you start.

People will generally feel positive towards your presentation if they believe it will meet their needs and expectations. A negative attitude might pervade for those who have been 'forced' to attend as well as those who do not understand why they have been invited. Negativity can also arise when people feel their schedule is under pressure and they haven't the time to attend. You will need to reassure these people that it will be worthwhile by giving them a personal WIIFM and invite positive people to counter-balance the influence they might exert.

How to build rapport

So what is rapport and why is it so important? Rapport is the building of a mutually respectful relationship – people with a rapport get along with each other. Establishing a quick rapport with your audience will encourage them to listen, if not wholeheartedly agree with your presentation.

> An under-pinning principle to rapport is that we like ourselves. So when we hear or see someone who says and does the things we would say and do, then we will like them as well.

So one of the simplest ways to build rapport is to start a presentation talking about things that the audience can relate to. For instance, if I know that the invitees are football fans, it might help if I can weave a story about football into my opening comments. Similarly, talking about 'increasing profits' during my opening comments to a Board of Directors not only makes sense but should encourage them to listen and support my primary aim.

The more you know about your audience, the easier it will be to build rapport.

Let's look at how this might work in practice – Consider *whether or not*:

- You would change the language in a presentation for teenagers from that used for senior citizens.
- You would choose a different perspective when presenting on, for instance, urban regeneration to one group from a depressed part of the country and another from an affluent part.
- You would choose different illustrations when discussing, for instance, ethics to two groups of opposing moral views.

There is a conflict here. It may be politically incorrect to treat people differently and yet you could fail in your primary aim if you treat them all the same. To treat audiences differently, we are presupposing that you can find out the profile of the audience in a politically correct (and legal) way. Political correctness would avoid any stereotyping of people by nature of their age, gender, race, belief system etc.

So how can you find out about your audience without stereotyping or offending anyone? Well you could ask them to tell you:

- Their favourite music or TV programmes
- If they were given three wishes, what would they be?
- Significant events in their life
- Three key words that describe themselves/their employer
- Their ambitions

Now I admit that these might look a bit weird and it would be even weirder if you sent out a questionnaire to solicit the answers. An informal yet cleverly worded chat with a few members of the audience can give you an idea of their attitude, personality, beliefs, age and motivations, without asking the questions you cannot ask, such as 'what do you believe?' or 'how old are you?' So think about what you would like to know in preparing for a specific presentation and then formulate just one or two such questions which will enable you discover how to build rapport.

WHAT MAKES A PRESENTATION GREAT?

Successfully incorporating ideas from other presenters and presentations as to what made them successful in the eyes of *this* audience, will increase the likelihood of your success. You can also learn from any bad experiences that they have had. If other presenters have worked with your audience previously, you can ask them about the feedback they received.

TOP TIPS

Do not attempt to be someone that you are not. Admiring the presentation style of Winston Churchill, John F Kennedy or whomever should never encourage you to attempt to mimic them. It will not work.

Successful presenters may be performers but they are not pretenders – their success is driven from bringing out the best of themselves rather than attempting to adopt the best of others. So learn from others' experiences and adapt that learning to your own style.

 ACTION POINT

Think about what you would like to know about your audience in advance, and how you are going to gather this information. For example in the case of the invitation to the launch of this book we could ask the audience to send back a form outlining what kind of presentation questions they would like answered and any details of the other *Successful* titles they would like to hear.

QUICK RECAP

- *Publish your primary aim to your audience whenever feasible and check that it will meet their expectations – before you start your preparation.*
- *If the subject of your presentation must remain confidential until the last minute, seek to manage the rumour and speculation that will occur.*
- *Invite not only those who are needed to support your primary aim but also those who might challenge it. Invite advocates of your primary aim who have the power and/ or influence to counteract any negativity.*
- *Pro-actively accommodate any special needs of the audience.*
- *Invitations to your presentation should offer incentives for individuals to attend (as well as stating the time, place etc). Give your audience a WIIFM.*
- *The more you know about your audience and their attitude towards your primary aim, the better you will be able to hone your message and, therefore, achieve success.*
- *Pitch the content of your presentation above the average knowledge level of the audience yet never assume they will understand terminology and jargon.*
- *Adapt the experiences of other successful presenters to suit your own style, but don't try to mimic presenters you admire.*

CHAPTER 4

Logistics and the location

A presenter's life would be so much easier, if only…

There are so many things that could make presenting easier, but high on the list for me would be perfect logistics.

Even if you have presented at a particular location many times in the past without difficulty, there are significant dangers in assuming that nothing can or will go wrong.

So what logistics should we plan for? And what should we do when the best laid plans go awry?

LUCKY ENOUGH TO CHOOSE?

A lucky presenter will be able to choose a location that is convenient for the audience, or at least the majority of them.

The chosen location may not necessarily be convenient to you but, as presenter, you have to make the extra effort since, you need them more than they need you (or your primary aim will not succeed). The most frequent culprits ignoring this convenience 'rule' are those who are into power games – that is, when they will ask 20 people to travel 100 miles to sit in a presentation at his or her office. This is not only childish but highly inefficient in terms of people's travelling time and costs.

A *really* lucky presenter will choose not only the location but also the specific room in which the presentation is to be made. Such a room should:

- Be of the right size for everyone to sit in a layout suited to your presentation.
- Give you, as presenter, a spacious 'stage' area for you and your equipment.
- Enable everyone to see and hear you and your visual aids.
- Have the necessary power supply and/or technology.
- Be free from distraction.
- Have heating and lighting controls that you can adjust.
- Be convenient for toilets and, if appropriate, have an area set aside for refreshments.
- Readily accommodate people with special needs.
- Follow Health and Safety guidelines at all times.

It has to be said, however, that it is very rare for presenters to have the ideal room and location for their presentations. Having determined what you would like, you must also consider how to *manage* a location which has either been given to you by others or, for whatever reason, simply failed to deliver your expectations. There is one overriding principle here: Be prepared for the unexpected!

TOP TIPS

Dos and Don'ts of location planning

- **DO** tell people what you specifically need from a location and room to support the successful delivery of your presentation.
- **DO NOT** assume that your needs will be met.
- **DO** visit the location before your presentation to allow for any necessary organisation (or re-organisation).
- **DO NOT** leave this to the last minute.
- **DO** ensure that all the logistics are managed before, during and after your presentation.
- **DO NOT** be inflexible in adapting to circumstance.

ARRANGING THE SPACE

Chairs and tables

Your primary aim will help you to determine which layout will be best. The most typical layouts are described respectively as the horse-shoe, boardroom, restaurant and theatre.

- The **horseshoe** (sometimes also called the 'C' or 'U' shape) is when the audience is arranged in an open-ended circle. This is great for encouraging discussions amongst the audience (although that means the presenter may have difficulty exercising control). It is unlikely to work for audiences of 20 or more.
- The **boardroom** is when the audience is arranged around one large table. This arrangement can be quite formal. It will only work successfully for small groups and, even then, can disrupt sight-lines between presenters and their audience.
- The **restaurant** (or café) layout is when the audience are arranged around a number of tables. This is particularly good when the presentation is mixed with group working. It can

work for large groups but again, watch out for interrupted sight-lines, between the audience, presenter and any visual aids.

- The **theatre** layout is when the audience is seated in staggered rows. This layout is most suited to large, formal events. Unfortunately, theatre style is sometimes used to squeeze the maximum number of people into a given room and it will inhibit audience participation.

Chairs can have a real impact on the success (or not) of a presentation. When my company opened a new training centre, it took a lot of searching to find chairs that, even after a couple of hours, remained comfortable. Small, intimate presentations might prompt you to think about using sofas and armchairs and, whilst some consider this appropriate, I tend to think it encourages people to fall asleep!

Tables could be included, especially when the audience needs to take or read notes. However, they can create an emotional and physical barrier between the audience and the presenter, which will not necessarily be conducive to creating the right atmosphere.

What to do if you don't get the layout you want

What if the layout won't fit in the room?

You could change the seating plan (theatre style takes up less space than a horseshoe for instance) or remove tables, providing it doesn't disrupt the achievement of your primary aim. Alternatively, you could split the audience into two 'sittings'.

What if the room is too large?

Try to define a lesser area within the room, perhaps with a temporary partition – even a row of chairs can show a 'boundary' line.

What if the chairs are uncomfortable?

Give people frequent breaks.

What if there are no chairs?

Strange as it might sound, I was told that an incoming Chief Executive of a British bank could never contact any of his senior staff because they were always in meetings. So he had all the furniture in the meeting rooms removed and issued instructions that the rooms could still be used, but no-one was allowed to lean against anything or sit on the floor. Meetings suddenly became much shorter! If you don't have the furniture, your presentation will have to be very brief. Think about how this will impact the structure of your presentation and your achievement of your primary aim.

What if there are chairs but no tables?

Consider providing your audience with clipboards.

Setting your 'stage'

Your 'stage' does not need to be a platform – it is simply the area within the room that you, as presenter, have reserved for yourself. Your primary aim will determine the appropriate staging, along with all the other logistics. Setting up your visual aids will be an important part of this and we are going to deal with this in a separate chapter, but what should we think about now?

Give yourself some space.

Good presenters will 'use' a stage to dramatic effect; a concert performer who takes the stage on their own doesn't ask for a one metre square stage, their performance is enhanced by their movement around the stage – and so it should be for you.

Set the right distance between you and the audience.

As a general guide, the centre of your staging area (that is, where you might typically stand) needs to be between two and three metres from the nearest member of the audience. Being too near them makes eye contact difficult and can make the people at the front feel uncomfortable. Being too far away could make it difficult to 'connect' with your audience, even more so if they can't see or hear you!

Avoid creating a barrier

Avoid, if at all possible, creating a barrier between you and the audience. Sitting behind a desk or using a lectern sends a very formal, controlling message to the audience and inhibits the ease by which you can establish rapport. However, you will need a table for your notes, a glass of water etc.

Decide if you want a chair or stool.

Sitting down can be particularly useful when you want to encourage participation by your audience (but be aware that by dropping your eye level to their height, you are effectively relinquishing a degree of control over the presentation).

Will the audience be able to see you?

Are they hidden behind a room's supporting pillars? Whatever seating plan you have for the audience, test out various seating positions to ensure that everyone will be able to see you and your visuals.

Can the audience hear you?

Do not shout out at the start of your presentation 'Can you hear me at the back?' Not only will it be too late to do anything about it if they can't, but you will probably not be able to maintain that volume throughout your presentation. So test the acoustics with a colleague in advance.

What to do if you haven't got the staging you want?

What if you are too cramped?

You could choose to sit down which would allow you to be physically closer to your audience without cramping them. You could also change the seating layout.

What if the audience cannot clearly see?

You could again change the layout but failing that, large-scale projected images of you and your visual aids will be required.

What if the audience might not be able to hear?

Again, changing the seating plan to bring the back row nearer to you could help. The alternative would be to use a microphone. When using a microphone run a test before the audience arrives, don't shout into it and know how to turn it off. (There have been many embarrassing tales of people with radio microphones going to the toilet with it still switched on!) If the microphone is static, try to avoid varying the distance between you and it.

OTHER PLANNING CONSIDERATIONS

Distractions and interruptions

An audience can easily get distracted. Just a few of the noisy examples that I have experienced include:

- A fight breaking out in an adjacent corridor
- Builders using pneumatic drills
- Fighter aircraft practising their low level flying overhead
- Piped music and loudspeaker announcements

What if any of these occur? Well, it is always useful to have an emergency contact at the location so you can quickly inform them that you need their help. You could also offer an impromptu break to the audience. Sometimes, a brief pause by the presenter to allow temporary noise to subside is all that is necessary – avoid trying to 'drown' out the distraction by shouting.

And some of the visual distractions I have witnessed are:

- Passers-by pulling faces at windows
- Awkwardly placed mirrors (on one occasion showing the back of a presenter's skirt caught in her underwear)
- Staring out of the window at a herd of deer
- Trainspotting

The trick here is to arrange the audience's seating to face away from windows or mirrors. If that is not feasible, consider closing blinds or simply using flip chart paper to blank out the view.

Other typical interruptions include:

- Fire alarms being sounded
- Mobile phones ringing
- Urgent messages

> If a fire alarm sounds, stop your presentation immediately and evacuate the building. All audiences should be made aware before a presentation starts of the evacuation routes and procedures.

I have found that asking people to turn off their mobile phones at the start of a presentation is increasingly resisted. They just get too stressed at the thought of being out of contact with their world even for a short time! I still ask for a comprehensive 'turn-off' but settle for the non-compliers to leave it on in silent mode and agree that, should it vibrate, they will leave the room. Take a similar approach for anyone receiving hand-written urgent messages.

Heat and light

The room temperature should be cool (but not cold), especially before you start since a crowded room will quickly warm up from body heat alone. A warm room will not only lure the audience to fall asleep, it will probably make you feel uncomfortable and you really don't want your audience to see you sweating!

The preferred level of lighting will be dependent on the type of any visual aid to be used and the needs of the people in the room. Whilst projected images work best in a darkened room (just like at the cinema) it may not be possible unless blinds or curtains can be drawn. Nor would darkened rooms make sense if the audience has to either make or refer to notes. One more thing to remember – don't make the room so dark that you can't read your own notes!

What if you cannot adjust the temperature?
Portable fans/heaters could help (if they comply with relevant Health and Safety requirements) but failing that, give people more than the typical number of breaks to cool down or warm up.

What if you cannot adjust the light level?
Projecting images with a dark background and lighter coloured lettering will be much easier to read (than the reverse colouring) in light rooms, as will placing a projector screen in front of a window.

Special needs

There are no 'what if' scenarios here: all rooms in all locations must be able to fulfil any special needs.

You will be inviting people who are needed to achieve your primary aim and if just one in a hundred cannot see, hear or assimilate the message, for whatever reason, you will fail. And you will have disrespected the entire audience, not just the individual concerned.

Health and Safety

Again, there are no 'what ifs' here, a location is either within the appropriate boundaries of Health and Safety or it isn't. And if it isn't, you mustn't use it. Remember, however, that whilst a room might start by meeting Health and Safety requirements, you could create a situation which causes the room to drop below standard. For instance, a room could become unusable if:

- The maximum capacity for a room is exceeded
- Fire exits are blocked or evacuation signs are covered up, deliberately or otherwise
- Loose cables are running across the floor

Additional space

It is possible that you will need more space than just the room in which your presentation is to be held. Consider:

• Where will your audience be welcomed? Do they need a place to sign-in or collect name badges?

• Where will any refreshments be served? (It can be very distracting if food and drink are brought into a room when you are mid-flow in your presentation – even more so when people return to clear the debris.)

• Where are the toilets? (This may sound too obvious a question, but one location I was offered required the audience to walk outside for 200 yards to the toilets and in mid-winter the weather was just too unreliable to make this a viable location.)

• Do you need break-out areas for small groups to work in before re-convening back in the main room?

 ACTION POINT

Using the primary aim you have developed over previous chapters:

• Determine where your forthcoming presentation should take place.

• What is the best layout? Include chairs, tables, staging etc.

• What, if any, additional areas will you need?

• Create a list of what you need to check before you commit to delivering your presentation in that location.

• If you already know the location will it support the achievement of your primary aim?

Timings

There are multiple timings to be considered and co-ordinate:

- From what time will the room be available?
- By what time can you reasonably expect your audience to arrive by?
- How much time should you give the audience between their arrival and when your presentation starts?
- How long will you need to create your preferred layout? Time should still be set aside in case you haven't got the layout someone promised to set up for you.
- How long will it take you to set up your staging and visual aids? Never assume that any technology is quick to set up!
- How long will you need to mentally prepare yourself, after you are satisfied that the logistics are all in place?
- What is the maximum time you need to achieve your primary aim? (If you undercut this time, it will generally be appreciated by an audience.)
- How much time should be set aside for answering questions?
- What will be the impact on your timetable of any breaks? Be realistic with this timing; it would not be unusual for the audience to take 20 minutes for a 10 minute interval.
- How long will it take to vacate the room when the presentation is finished?
- Would the latest anticipated finish time suit the audience's follow-on commitments? (For instance: will public transport still be available to get them home?)
- If you add up all the timings above, will the room be available for all of the time you need?

ACTION POINT

Continuing from the earlier Action Point on p.52.
Create a comprehensive and realistic timetable for your location.

SECURING YOUR NEEDS

It is highly advisable to itemise the logistics in writing if you are also responsible for booking the location. Consider:

- How much will it all cost? (Watch for add-on costs such as tea/coffee or equipment hire.)
- Will the room be set up to your specification before your arrival?
- Who can help if you need to change anything? (Ask for specific names.)
- What are the cancellation charges?

Ensure you get written confirmation of all the details you have agreed.

TOP TIPS

The scale of logistical planning and its fulfilment on the day is substantial. Get some help! Can others:

- Thoroughly brief and book the location?
- Welcome your audience?
- Be available on the day to manage any last minute changes or distractions?
- Help with the setting up and dismantling of the stage area?
- Shield you from the logistics to enable you to mentally prepare to deliver a positive presentation?

QUICK RECAP

- *Logistics need detailed planning, but never assume that your plans will work perfectly.*
- *Locations should be chosen by balancing convenience (for the audience) and the overall cost-effectiveness.*
- *Your primary aim will have a direct impact on determining the appropriate layout of the room, which in turn will dictate the size of room required.*
- *Your audience should be made comfortable, but not too comfortable. Think about the type of seating and whether or not tables are desirable.*
- *Develop the staging area to enable rapport building, not least by ensuring that the presenter and visual aids can be seen and heard by every member of the audience.*
- *Be prepared to manage unwanted distractions and interruptions.*
- *Seek to achieve the right levels of temperature and lighting.*
- *Always pay attention to special needs and Health and Safety requirements.*
- *Don't restrict your planning to just preparing the room for your presentation, consider other areas that you and your audience will need to use.*
- *Create a timetable from the moment that the room becomes available until it has to be cleared.*
- *Communicate your logistical needs in writing.*
- *Recruiting on-site logistics help can be invaluable to respond to unforeseen circumstances.*
- *If your primary aim cannot be achieved in the location, for whatever reason, either change the location or scale down what you planned to achieve.*

CHAPTER 5

Creating a structure

The mind wanders. With the best will in the world, it happens to us all – we daydream, we get bored, we think about what else we might be doing. And that's okay – a good presenter will *know* that the audience won't listen to every word, but even the best presenters will not always know *when* their audience has stopped listening, although snoring would be a major clue!

The challenge for this chapter to address is how you can help your audience to understand the presentation even when they have temporarily stopped listening and – in the extreme – how we can avoid them giving up entirely on a presentation because they missed a key part. The answer lies in developing a structure that the audience can readily follow, even for very short, small-scale presentations.

STRUCTURE

We will start by looking at how books are structured and draw from that how we might develop an effective structure for your presentations.

Books are divided into chapters, chapters into paragraphs and paragraphs into sentences. The first few chapters of a novel will introduce the key things or characters you need to understand the rest of the book, until the closing chapters when everything is consolidated. When reading this book on presentations, you also have headings to guide you through the text and help you to find your place easily whenever you break off from reading. This division, this structure, is designed to help you, the reader, understand the information within the book. Similarly, your presentation will need a structure to help your audience to understand and re-connect to your presentation should they lose track.

There needs to be a proper introduction to your topic, a middle which includes your key message(s) and a formal end to a presentation which consolidates everything you have said.

How to develop a structure

At this point, we will bring together much of our earlier preparatory work.

You will need to draw on the work already covered in this book to develop an effective structure. Namely:
- Defining the primary aim.
- Determining what you must, should and could communicate.
- The level of knowledge of the intended audience (which includes the degree to which they understand terminology).
- The size of your audience.
- The seating layout you are going to use for your presentation.
- How much time you will have for the presentation.

Each of the bullet points become interconnected at this stage. For instance, the knowledge level of the audience (or lack of it) will dictate the information you **must** communicate. And what you must, should and could communicate will be restricted by the time you have available. Further, we have already determined that the size of your audience will influence the seating layout, and both of these factors will restrict the various structural options you might have to achieve your primary aim. For example, very large audiences restrict the opportunity for a high level of audience participation.

All presentations must have a beginning, middle and end irrespective of your chosen structure.

THE BEGINNING

What must be in the beginning?

So where do you start? To help, let's look at how Cathy, a teacher, started to develop a presentation for parents about a forthcoming school trip.

An eight-point checklist for what must be included in the beginning of your presentation:	Cathy's key points:
A welcome, a greeting.	Good afternoon.
Introduce yourself.	My name is Cathy.
State your credentials for presenting this topic. Be brief.	The school's history teacher and organiser of the potential trip.
Outline what you want to achieve (from your primary aim). You are unlikely to declare all your success criteria.	To enable parents to make a reasoned decision as to whether or not they want their children to go on the proposed trip.

How long it will take.	20 minutes.
Give people a 'wake-up' call to get them listening: a WIIFM.	Going on this trip could make all the difference to each child's examination results.
Your approach, your structure, your 'headings' for the middle of your presentation.	To describe four key elements: the trip itself, how it will help the examination results, the logistics and the next steps.
When you would like any questions.	At the end.

What other information should or could be in the beginning?

Depending on the situation, you might include:

- Domestic arrangements such as the evacuation procedures, the toilets, break times, refreshment arrangements, smoking rules and how messages for the audience will be dealt with.

- A request to your audience, for the benefit of all, to turn off their mobile phones.

- Background to the presentation. Although not essential, it may be useful for the audience to know why the presentation is being made. (If this cannot be done briefly, consider making it the first point in the middle part of the structure.)

- The information sources upon which your presentation is based.

- Whether or not you intend to distribute any supporting materials, and, if so, when.

- Checking (which you should already know if you have prepared fully) that everyone can see and hear clearly.

- To dispel your nerves, it *can* be useful to encourage some involvement by the audience at an early stage, perhaps by asking them a question. Think about this carefully, will you recover if no-one gives you the answers you want?

Developing the script

Having determined everything that is needed in the beginning of your presentation, you can now add some linking phrases and words to create the beginning of your script:

Let's take another look at Cathy's presentation to see how she developed her script.

'Welcome everyone and thank you for coming along this afternoon. My name is Cathy, your children's History teacher and organiser of a proposed student trip to the Tower of London. I would like to take just 20 minutes of your time to describe the trip itself before moving on to explain why I believe it will make all the difference to your children's history examination results this year, as well as being an uplifting experience in its own right. We'll also look at the logistics, schedule and the next steps I would ask of you so that I can, if you so wish, plan the trip in detail. If you have any questions, if you could please ask them at the end of the presentation, unless that is, you have any immediate questions now?'

There are fewer than 140 words in this introduction and yet it has 'weaved' together all the information required in the checklist. In particular, Cathy included the four key areas she **must** communicate if you didn't spot them: the trip itself, improved examination results (the WIIFM), the logistics and the next steps. Within her stated 20 minute timescale, four key parts to the middle of the presentation is probably all Cathy could realistically hope to achieve without overloading the audience.

Cathy later added information to the beginning that she believed she should or could include – the school's evacuation procedure, directions to the toilets and that the children hadn't been told of the trip to avoid potential emotional blackmail!

Developing your style

Although the style of Cathy's presentation may not yet be innovative (which we will outline in more detail in the next chapter) it has introduced a specific style.

Adopting a conversational style brings your personality into a presentation.

A conversational style says 'these are my words, not a script I dragged off a shelf' which makes it an original presentation (decreasing any possibility that the audience think that they will have heard it all before). Furthermore, by using her own style and words, Cathy will feel more comfortable, less nervous and, if Cathy is at ease, her audience will be as well. Note, however, that not all presentation topics are suited to this style – it will not work successfully, for example, at formal events when 'bad' news is being delivered.

TOP TIPS

Don't skimp on the beginning.

It gives people time to adjust to your voice and settle into your presentation.

ACTION POINT

Choose a topic for a forthcoming (or imaginary) presentation that you have to make. Then follow this guide to develop the beginning of the presentation:

• Use the checklist to note down what you **must** include in the beginning.

• Add to these notes what you should or could, if necessary, include.

• Write the beginning of your script in a conversational style.

THE MIDDLE

There are many ways to structure the middle of a presentation. Here, we will look a one straightforward approach which sorts the information under key headings and then presents them in a logical order. We will explore other, more innovative, options in the next chapter.

Continuing with her preparation, Cathy added the first of her key 'must communicate' headings. Then, she sorted (from her research) information that she **should** or **could** include under that heading, and this was how it started to shape up:

What must I include to achieve my primary aim?	What should I include to excel in achieving my primary aim?	What could I include that would support my primary aim?
The beginning		
The eight point checklist: • Welcome. • Your credentials. • What you want to achieve. • How long you will take.	From the 'what else?' list earlier: • The school's evacuation procedures. • How to find the toilets.	• There's no pressure, even the children haven't been told, to prevent any emotional blackmail they might use.
The middle		
• The trip to the Tower of London.	• Trips bring history 'alive', they make it real and practical. • The itinerary including visits to areas not normally open to the public.	• Stories of intrigue, murder and stored treasure. • Reminders of trips the parents might have gone on when they were at school.

In this book, headings guide you through the text and we need a similar approach when building a presentation. Such headings are called 'signposts' and are introduced between each key section to help anyone to re-start their listening if, for whatever reason, they have lost track of your presentation.

> All structures need signposts which summarise the last point made before introducing the next.

So Cathy added her signposting:

What must I include?	What should I include?	What could I include?
The beginning		
A beginning using the eight point checklist, for example: • Welcome. • Your credentials. • What you want to achieve. • How long you will take.	From the 'what else?' list earlier: • The school's evacuation procedures. • How to find the toilets.	• There's no pressure, even the children haven't been told, to prevent any emotional blackmail they might try.
Signpost: So that's what I am going to cover. Now let's talk about where I propose your children should visit.		
The Middle		
• The trip to the Tower of London.	• Trips bring history 'alive', they make it real and practical. • The itinerary including visits to areas not normally open to the public.	• Stories of intrigue, murder and stored treasure. • Reminders of trips the parents might have gone on when they were at school.

> **Signpost:** I'm sure we can all agree that the children will have a great time exploring the Tower of London, but let's not lose sight of the fact that it is designed to help them excel at their history examinations. (This signpost repeats the WIIFM Cathy mentioned in the beginning of her presentation.)

✍ ACTION POINT

Develop the middle of your presentation:

- Identify the headings that you must communicate (which should have already been mentioned in your introduction)
- Note under each heading what you must, should and could include
- Write down the linking signposts between each heading

THE ENDING

Having finished the main part of your presentation, there must be one last signpost that summarises all of the key headings you have covered, albeit with some 'hype' – and indicates that you are drawing to a close. What else must you include in the end?

- Any conclusions or recommendations that can be drawn from your presentation.
- A re-statement of your primary aim and that it has been achieved (do not express doubt – you must convey the belief that you have succeeded!).
- Repetition of the WIIFMs.
- An emphasis on what you want the audience to do as a result of the presentation.
- Sources of further information on the subject.
- A thank you to the audience for listening.
- An opportunity for questions (how to handle questions will be covered later).

Taking questions after you have finished your presentation can be dangerous since if the last question (or your answer) is in any way negative, it could destroy everything you have sought to achieve in your presentation. So pre-script some possible final comments to make when questions have finished.

> Always – but always – have the last word when presenting to ensure that it ends on a highly positive note.

How did Cathy plan to signpost and then close her presentation? Let's see:

> *'So to summarise the key points, the proposed trip to the Tower of London is going to give your children an insight that no ordinary tourist will gain, an insight that can only help them in their forthcoming examinations. The logistics for the day will be carefully planned to ensure that the safety of your children is paramount and, should you agree, we would ask that you let the school know by noon this Friday whether you would like your child to attend. I am happy, along with the head teacher who has been sitting quietly at the back of the room, to take any questions that you can think of now, but please do feel free to contact the school with any later questions that you might think of, however small they may appear. I would like to thank you on behalf of the head teacher, the school and myself for coming along and being such an attentive audience, always a great experience for a teacher, and would now ask if anyone has any questions.'*

And after the questions had all been answered, Cathy planned to add:

> *'I'm certain that this will be one of those major experiences that your children will remember in years to come. We can all look forward not only to stimulating their interest but also their exam results in what I believe will be an enjoyable learning experience. Thank you once again for listening and have a safe journey home.'*

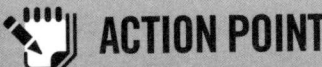 **ACTION POINT**

Develop the last part of your presentation:

• Determine the last signpost.

• Use the checklist to identify what you must, should and could include in the ending.

• Write the end of your presentation including your closing comments to end on a high.

ALLOCATING TIME

The overall time of your presentation has been determined in your primary aim. Now, you need to divide that time up in a balanced way. There are a number of reasons for doing this:

• Too short an introduction fails to give your audience time to 'tune-in' to your voice and settle into the style of your presentation.

• If the first of four key headings in the middle part of your presentation takes 30 minutes, someone in the audience will calculate that with three further headings, it could take another 90 minutes. As a result, they are likely to lose interest.

• Spending too much time on the earlier headings could mean that you will have to skip or rush the latter parts.

• Talking for too long may reduce the opportunity for questions – cynics amongst the audience will think that you did this deliberately.

• An audience may resent a presentation over running – they could miss transport links or their next appointment. For that reason alone, they may reject your presentation.

It would be wrong to be too prescriptive here, but as general guide on how to allocate time for a 20 minute presentation with four key headings in the middle:

The beginning	3 minutes
Each heading except the last one	2 minutes each = 6 minutes
The last heading	1 and a half minutes
The end (before questions)	3 minutes
Questions	5 minutes
Your closing comment	30 seconds
Total	**19 minutes**

How to get your timing right

Giving your headings roughly an equal amount of time says they are equally important. If one is going to take a disproportionate amount of time, you need to divide them into more than one heading. The last heading in the middle part is shorter because the audience knows you are on your last key point and will have slightly less patience.

As a minimum state what you must communicate and preferably what you should say. If time permits, add what you could say. Never miss out any of your key headings. Finishing your presentation a little earlier than planned will generally be well received by your audience.

TOP TIPS Leaving your audience wanting a little more from your presentation is better than giving them too much.

PULLING IT ALL TOGETHER

We can now bring together all the points in this chapter to create the structure for your presentation. In Cathy's example of the proposed school trip, it looked like this:

The proposed trip to the Tower of London	
The beginning	**3 minutes**

'Welcome everyone and thank you for coming along this afternoon. My name is Cathy, your children's History teacher and organiser of a proposed student trip to the Tower of London. I would like to take just 20 minutes of your time to describe the trip itself before moving on to expalin why I believe it will make all the difference to your children's history examination results this year as well as being an uplifting experience in its own right. We'll also look at the logistics, schedule and the next steps I would ask of you so that I can, if you so wish, plan the trip in detail. If you have any questions, please ask them at the end of the presentation, unless that is, you have any immediate questions now?'

I should add:	And I could say:
• The school's evacuation procedures. • How to find the toilets.	• There's no pressure, the children haven't been told, to prevent any emotional blackmail they might use.

Signpost: So that's what I am going to cover. Now let's talk about where I propose your children should visit.

The middle 1. The trip to the Tower of London		2 minutes
What must I include?	**What should I include?**	**What could I include?**
• Details about the trip to the Tower of London.	• Trips bring history 'alive', making it real and practical. • The itinerary including visits to areas not normally open to the public.	• Stories of intrigue, murder and stored treasure. • Reminders of trips the parents might have gone on when they were at school.

Signpost: I'm sure we can all agree that the children will have a great time exploring the Tower of London, but let's not lose sight of the fact that it is designed to help them excel at their history examinations.

The middle 2. Your children's examination results		2 minutes
What must I include?	**What should I include?**	**What could I include?**
• The potential positive impact in relation to your children's examination results.	• The connection between the Tower's history and school examination. • Statistics from previous students who have or have not gone on the trip before sitting the examination.	• A personal story by Cathy that describes how Cathy achieved 'average' history exam results until, in her case, she was guided around the Roman remains in Chester.

Signpost: So – to get those brilliant examination results, we need to make sure that everything is planned in detail...

The middle 3. The logistics		2 minutes
What must I include?	**What should I include?**	**What could I include?**
• Well organised logistics.	• The date, timings and cost. • Student:Teacher ratios. • Insurance.	• The school has run many trips over the years, all without incident.

Signpost: You can see that we try to think of everything to make it go smoothly, so how do we move this forward?

The middle 4. The next steps		1 and a half minutes
What must I include?	**What should I include?**	**What could I include?**
• The necessary next steps	• A deadline for enrolment • The school will then write to every parent	

The end (starting with a signpost)	3 minutes

'So to summarise the key points, the proposed trip to the Tower of London is going to give your children an insight that no ordinary tourist will gain, an insight that can only help them in their forthcoming examinations. The logistics for the day will be carefully planned to ensure that the safety of your children is paramount and, should you agree, we would ask that you let the school know by noon this Friday whether you would like your child to attend. I am happy – along with the head teacher who has been sitting quietly at the back of the room – to take any questions that you can think of now, but please do feel free to contact the school with any later questions that you think of – however small they may appear. I would like to thank you on behalf of the head teacher, the school and myself for coming along and being such an attentive audience – always a great experience for a teacher – and would now ask if anyone has any questions...'

Take questions	5 minutes
Closing comment	30 seconds

'I'm certain that this will be one of those major experiences that your children will remember in years to come. We can all look forward not only to stimulating their interest but also their exam results in what I believe will be an enjoyable learning experience. Thank you once again for listening and have a safe journey home.'

ACTION POINT

Use Cathy's structure to help you complete the development of your presentation.

 **QUICK RECAP**

- *Remember that the audience will not be listening to every word so you need to make it easy for them to 'reconnect' with your presentation with a clear structure and signposts.*
- *Thorough research is an essential step to creating a structure.*
- *All structures have a beginning, middle and end and in each part, there is information that you must, should or could communicate.*
- *A straightforward approach to structuring a presentation is to have a logical sequence of key points of roughly equal duration – but not too many to cause information overload.*
- *Divide the available time for your presentation between the points you wish to make.*
- *Close on a highly positive statement.*

CHAPTER 6

A more innovative approach to structure

If all presentations were created using the same structure, it wouldn't take long for you to become very bored. This is not to say that the logical approach described in the previous chapter is wrong – it can and does work very well – but that we need to explore how to create something that is different. So now we will look at a number of structural approaches to ensure that the audience can not only follow our presentation, but also enjoy the variety that we adopt to achieve our primary aim.

KEY STRUCTURAL PRINCIPLES

Whichever structural format you choose, there are key principles that you must always remember:

- Stay focused on achieving your primary aim.
- All presentations must have a beginning and an end.
- Signposts must be included.

TOP TIPS

If you cannot achieve your primary aim by making three or four key points (be it to persuade, influence, promote, analyse or whatever), your audience are unlikely to be swayed by a fifth or sixth point.

Suggested outlines for a 20 minute presentation using each of the proposed structures are given towards the end of the chapter.

CREATIVE STRUCTURES

The picture painter

There is a phrase 'a picture is worth a thousand words' and, visual aids aside, you can adapt this concept to structure your presentation. Let's look at both a wrong, and a right, way of using this structure:

> *'This house was, and is, the house of my dreams. It's got everything I could ever want... it has lawns, a long drive, massive kitchen and a huge master bedroom suite...'*

This may be brief, but it centres on the presenter's personal observations and fails to bring 'alive' the scene to the audience. So let's start to 'paint a picture':

> *'Imagine yourself driving towards tall wrought iron gates – black and so decorated with swags and leaves that you can hardly see*

through to the other side. But at a touch of a button, a button discreetly placed at the side of your steering wheel, those gates swing back to reveal a sweeping drive, gently curving its way through a lawn so lush, so green, so evenly trimmed, that a manicurist couldn't have done better.

'So through the wrought iron gates and along that curving drive amidst sweeping lawns you drive on to arrive at...'

Here the presenter is using the picture painting technique to good effect, describing each element in turn as it unfolds before the eye. The second paragraph summarised the scene so far before moving on to describe the house. The principle is that the audience will actually 'see' and therefore understand much more than the words alone could convey, because their imagination will embellish the picture from their own viewpoint. The only danger with this structure is that their imagination might end up conjuring a totally different image in their minds to that which the presenter is seeking to create; is the house at the end of the drive a ruin or a palace?

This structure is particularly useful when there is no obvious sequence to the presentation's content.

The story teller

Myths, legends, fairy-tales all carry a message that the writer wants the reader to learn. And for those of us who might struggle to readily grasp that meaning, many add the phrase 'and the moral of the story is...' I can remember many of the stories that were read to me as a child, although I might have to think a little more to recall the moral or the advocated behaviour that such stories were designed to instil. So the good and the not-so-good news about this structure is that the audience might love the story but miss the point entirely. Keeping that in mind, let's see how this might work...

'I went to the supermarket on the way home from work yesterday. Now I hadn't shopped in this particular supermarket before but I

guess I thought that the service would be okay and I could get out reasonably quick. How wrong I was!

'First the trolley – one of those you have to disconnect from a chain by inserting a coin – swallowed my coin but gripped like fury to the chain. I pulled and kicked the trolley, scuffing my new shoes in the process and got nowhere. And the trolley collectors – the staff who collect all the trolleys up – they all disappeared. I could swear there were at least four such staff in the car park when I first arrived.

'So what did I do? I looked for the manager or a supervisor or, well, anyone, in uniform. Everyone was busy doing something and then I spotted the customer service desk. 'Yes', I think, 'this will sort it'. So with a determined look, I walked towards the desk and, just as I was within shouting distance – yes, you guessed it – the staff started talking on their mobiles. Now I was mad!'

So what do you think the presenter was trying to achieve? There are a wide range of possibilities: Causes of stress? Never wear new shoes to the supermarket? Improve 'trolley' staff rosters? Ban mobiles at work? It could have been any or all of these or something totally different. So to ensure that your story still achieves your primary aim:

- Keep the story simple and dismiss any part that bears no relation to your primary aim.
- Be prepared to elaborate, invent, re-sequence, change or merge multiple stories to achieve your goal.
- Use signposts to summarise and then remind the audience of your primary aim. In the example above, the true purpose would have been revealed if I added at the end of each paragraph: 'So how do you think this supermarket is doing now to fulfil its promise of offering an excellent customer service?'

- Be absolutely certain the story can be told within your allotted time. You cannot stop before you reach the end.

The advertiser

Television advertisements are a form of presentation and we can adapt the structure that is used in many of them. Let's look at how, for instance, a car might be promoted on television in a 30 second slot:

- In the opening seconds, there is a 'wake-up' call (or WIIFM) to the target audience – perhaps music from a certain era. If the music appeals to you, you have been targeted by the advertiser and, if it works, you will watch the rest of the advert. If the music is not to your liking, the advertiser is happy for you to leave the room.
- The next stage of the advert will show the car doing exactly what the target audience would want from a car. Perhaps superb road holding when taking a hairpin bend at speed. It might also show the car on an empty road, the subliminal message being 'buy this car and you'll never get stuck in traffic again'.
- The advertiser will then try to anticipate any cynical comments from its target audience, what are termed as 'objections' and, without actually mentioning them, will seek to negate them. So if the audience suspects that taking hair-pin bends at speed forces the driver to sway from side to side, the driver will be shown sitting very comfortably as the car navigates the bends.
- The advert will, in the closing seconds, heavily brand the car (so you don't mistakenly buy a competitor's) and seek to close a deal, perhaps with a special price or free extras.

This structure will only be successful if you *know* what your audience wants. If you get your research wrong, the audience will disconnect from your presentation very quickly.

FACTUAL STRUCTURES

The persuader

This structure seeks to make the outcome of the presentation so inevitable that it cannot be disputed. To be successful with this approach, you must exclude from the beginning and middle anything that can be questioned or challenged by:

* Talking exclusively about 'facts' and 'absolutes'.
* Avoiding words like 'I' or 'my' (because it must be totally de-personalised).
* Signposting the end by summarising the key facts/absolutes and then stating the conclusion as the only possible outcome.

In chapter two, we laid the foundations for this structure by classifying our research using FACTOR (F for fact; A for absolutes; C for conclusions; T for tenets; O for opinions; R for reactions). We also looked at how the politician's statement: 'I think we should go to war' could be far more persuasive if the argument was centred on facts and absolutes. This is also a useful technique to use in your presentation structure to convince your audience that the facts you have presented are undeniably true.

The seller

Here, the presenter poses a series of questions (no less than four) to which the audience are (almost) inevitably going to agree. Here is a simplified example:

1. Have you experienced rising heating bills over the last few years?
2. Do you expect those heating bills to rise over the next few years?
3. Would you like to reduce your heating bills and save money?
4. If I could offer you a solution to these heating issues, would you be interested?

On the basis that you have mentally said 'yes' to the questions above, the presenter then adds: 'So you must arrange to double glaze your home today and I can help you with that...'

And before you discard this as being only appropriate to sell something...

Promoting your ideas is the same as selling a product or service.

This approach can be used to take a negative stance against a given topic. Politicians, for instance, could use this structure to develop an argument as to why the audience should not vote for their opponents. In my opinion, it's not a particularly attractive option, but if you do use it, it is better to attack the person's ideas rather than the person themselves. For instance, it would be better to say: 'These economic plans are a recipe for disaster' rather than 'John's economic plans are a disaster'.

The onion peeler

The onion peeler is particularly (but not exclusively) useful in presentations that analyse a situation or problem. We'll move straight to a brief example:

> 'Our clothing sales in the last quarter are disappointing – a 5% decrease on last year. In fact, this decrease is in the sales of men's clothing since the other departments are achieving sales level or better than last year. If we take a closer look at menswear, we actually find that it is the casual-wear sales that are so disappointing. On yet further analysis, we find that the sales of denim jeans have plummeted by over 10%, a figure that has been disguised by sales improvements in other sections of the men's department...'

Naturally, such content would need to be substantiated by more detailed statistics. So this structure removes every 'layer' of the problem until you find the underlying problem, like peeling back onion layers until you reach the core.

Typically, such a presentation would be followed by a discussion to determine an appropriate remedy of the specific problem identified.

This structure could be also used in reverse by describing how a given situation was improved (layer one) and how that layer was improved further (layer two) and so on to describe how a qualitative outcome was achieved – a different analogy would be a series of building blocks which are dependent upon their foundations.

The sniper

Addressing an issue or problem from one perspective can work. For example: you could make a presentation on why people shouldn't take illegal drugs because of the long-term health damage they can cause.

The sniper, however, enhances this approach by attacking an issue from multiple, unrelated angles on the basis that if the first 'shot' doesn't work, maybe the second or third will. So a presentation to deter drug taking will, perhaps, make four separate points: such as damage to health; social and family breakdown; financial desperation and the slippery slope towards crime.

The reveal

Here we reveal at the start of the presentation the conclusions or recommendations that the presentation is designed to justify. A simple version of this structure is to create a chronological structure but to declare the goal that was achieved at the start of the presentation. For example:

> 'Today, we launched a manned space rocket that will, over the coming months, travel to Mars…and I'm going to explain how, after years of research and devoted effort by an outstanding team of people, we achieved a goal only dreamed off just a few short years ago.'

It doesn't even have to be a chronological structure:

'My name is Brian Lomas, author of Successful Presentations. *It is often said that there is at least one book inside each of us just itching to get out and today we are going to cover four key activities that you can take to get your "itch" published...'*

A typical use of this structure is when you are applying for a new job; the beginning of your presentation would declare not only that you want the job (your primary aim) but also that you are the right person to do it (the reveal). Your presentation would then declare the attitude, skills, experience and qualities that you offer before closing with the message that you have just proven that you will excel in the job.

This leads us on to two structures that are specifically designed to initiate a discussion about the need for change, even when you don't actually know what that change should be.

DISCUSSIONS FOR CHANGE

The global change

Organisations need to change to keep up in an ever changing world – to stand still in a competitive environment is to get left behind. How many companies do you know of that still only manufacture typewriters in today's computer world?

To initiate a discussion on change – even if you do know what that change should be – you can 'set-the-scene' by describing the four 'global' drivers for change:

- Economic factors include the drive for value for money and cost efficiency. They include an assessment of the economic cycle and resultant availability of money and cash flow.
- Environmental factors embrace the whole concept of 'going green' – global warming, waste and resource management, creating and maintaining healthy workplaces etc.
- Social factors primarily relate to the changing expectations of people and the societies within which they live. So there is a wide range of issues that could be included here, human

rights (including the right to privacy) increasing customer expectations, improved quality of life and healthcare.

• Technological factors include automation, the internet, computers and the increasing dependency on technology for the most basic of our needs.

Using these four elements for the middle part of your presentation will open the way for a discussion on what needs to change.

However, bear in mind that it would not be unusual for factors to appear contradictory. As a condensed example, if presenting to a chain of travel agents, it could be said that:

'Over the next decade, it is anticipated that oil prices will rise dramatically (economic) as global demand outstrips supply. Despite this, industries that use the oil (and airlines are just one of them) are being urged to take account of demands by the public (social) to reduce carbon emissions (environmental). Such environmental concerns amongst the public could stimulate a decline in long haul flights despite (a potential contradiction) the increasing (social) demands for a work:life balance and more time away from the workplace. Technical advances in airline fuel efficiency are progressing at a rate faster than anytime since the last world war (technological), yet the aeroplanes that we charter today, and in the immediate future, will not benefit from such advances. What should, what must, we do to grow our business in the face of such challenges?'

(For the record: Please do not infer I know about future oil prices, future demand for oil, carbon emission levels, technical advances etc. I'm merely trying to illustrate a point.)

The local change

This structure uses an analysis tool called 'SWOT' accredited to the late Albert S. Humphrey of Stanford University and again can be used to instigate a discussion on change. SWOT stands for:

• Strengths: What internal strengths does our organisation have?

- Weaknesses: What internal weaknesses are there within the organisation?
- Opportunities: What external opportunities present themselves?
- Threats: What external threats are there to our organisation?

These four key headings can be used to present an overview of the issues facing an organisation. The goal will be capitalise upon the strengths, convert the weaknesses into strengths (or mitigate them), seize the (key) opportunities and counter or manage the threats. For example a SWOT analysis for a restaurant may conclude:

> *'Our restaurant has a loyal customer base (strength) amongst people between the ages of 25 and 35 who are prepared to pay for our organic and locally-grown food. However, we face increasing difficulty (weakness) on sourcing such foods on an on-going basis, which can result in customer disappointment when items on our menus are withdrawn almost on a daily basis. The town's new transport links have increased our potential customer base (opportunity) but has equally given our customers ease of access to our competitors (threat). What must we do?'*

COMBINING MULTIPLE STRUCTURES

It may be tempting at this point to say that you would like to use a bit of this structure and a bit of that and maybe a little of another, but it is likely to cause confusion. However, you can use different structures for two presentations that are divided by, for instance, a coffee-break. Indeed, using the same structure throughout a day of presentations would be very boring to witness, if not to present.

For longer presentations (say over 40 minutes), you could, with care, use one overall structure but within each key heading of the middle section, adopt ways to structure each point. For example: on one point you could tell a story and on another you could paint a picture and it should work well because they are both creative structures. Some structural combinations will not work so well. For example: the picture painting and factual based persuasion do not combine well. The former requires the audience to be creative, a mindset you definitely don't want when you introduce facts. It's too dramatic a change for the audience in how they are expected to assimilate the information.

 **ACTION POINT**

Think of three different presentation topics. Identify at least two different structures for each presentation (don't forget to consider the logical approach of the last chapter).

Then choose the structure that you believe will work best, having considered the following:

- Your primary aim (some of the advocated structures are designed to achieve specific purposes, for example: the onion peeler and sniper are for presentations of an analysis).
- How formal/informal will the presentation be and how serious a topic is it? (Some structures, such as a telling a story, are better suited to informal, relatively light-hearted presentations.)
- What does your audience already know about the subject? (The more they know, the more creative you could be.)
- Does the environment in which you are delivering the presentation offer any ideas or restrictions?

	Paint a picture	Story telling	Advertise	Persuade	Sell	Peel an onion	Sniper	Reveal	Global change	Local change
Introduction	✓	✓	✓	✓	✓	✓	✓	✓	✓	✓
Signpost	✓	✓	✓	✓	✓	✓	✓	✓	✓	✓
Middle										
Heading 1	Paint a bit	Tell a bit	Benefit 1	Fact or Absolute 1	Question 1	Layer 1	Attack 1	1st step	Economy	Strength
Signpost	✓	✓	✓	✓	✓	✓	✓	✓	✓	✓
Heading 2	Paint a bit more	Tell a bit more	Benefit 2	Fact or absolute 2	Question 2	Layer 2	Attack 2	2nd step	Environment	Weakness
Signpost	✓	✓	✓	✓	✓	✓	✓	✓	✓	✓
Heading 3	Paint yet more	Tell yet more	Benefit 3	Fact or absolute 3	Question 3	Layer 3	Attack 3	3rd step	Social	Opportunity
Signpost	✓	✓	✓	✓	✓	✓	✓	✓	✓	✓
Heading 4	Complete the picture	Finish the story	Negate the cynical	Fact or absolute 4	Question 4	Layer 4	Attack 4	4th step	Technology	Threat
Signpost	✓	✓	✓	✓	✓	✓	✓	✓	✓	✓
End	✓	✓	✓	✓	✓	✓	✓	✓	✓	✓
Questions *	✓	✓	✓	✓	✓	✓	✓	✓	✓	✓
Closing hype	✓	✓	✓	✓	✓	✓	✓	✓	✓	✓

* Unless questions are taken throughout your presentation

QUICK RECAP

- *Whatever structure you adopt, make sure you stay on track with your primary aim.*
- *All presentations should have some form of structure including a beginning, middle and end along with appropriate signposting.*
- *Having lots of multiple points within the middle section of your presentation is increasing the possibility that your audience will become confused.*
- *Combining too many different structures in the same presentation is exceptionally difficult and not to be recommended.*

CHAPTER 7

Scripts, prompts and making it memorable

Think of your favourite songs. Chances are you will listen to them many, many times. Why? Well, because you enjoy them, because they are good, because they are memorable – but how would you feel if the words were different every time you heard them? Well it certainly wouldn't be memorable anymore! So a successful songwriter must craft the words (and tune) with great care. They will try different words and phrases until they find that memorable message their audiences crave and then they stick to it. And it's the same for presenters.

The words must be tried, tested, sifted, selected and, most importantly, written down to create a presentation that not only achieves a primary aim but creates that memorable experience.

A SCRIPT

The pros

Reciting a script verbatim (word by word) has a number of key advantages:

- You can deliver a *precise* message. For example: a script would be essential when every word is important, perhaps when presenting to the press.
- Your message will be *consistent*. Delivering a verbatim script will ensure total consistency if you have to make the same presentation on more than one occasion.
- You can deliver a *complete* message. If you read from a script, nothing will be missed.
- You can *rehearse* it. Successful presenters always rehearse what they are going to say – even those who appear to be speaking 'off-the-cuff' have worked out their words in advance. If the words change every time you rehearse, you will have no idea whether or not you have got it 'right'.
- You can *time* it. In the last chapter we talked about breaking down a 20 minute presentation into two and three minute slots. You could squeeze over 300 words into two minutes but it would be a big mistake – assuming, that is, you want your audience to hear and understand what you are saying. (To illustrate this, time yourself reading aloud the first four bullet points above. There are 120 words and if it takes you less than a minute, you are talking too fast for a presentation.)
- You can *manage a potential fear*. Do you fear your mind 'going blank' during your presentation? A script *can* help you to manage that fear – you can look at your script and start speaking again. In your panic, however, the challenge will be to find where you are up to and that is not always easy.

And, most importantly:

- A script will ensure that you will *achieve your primary aim*; assuming the script has been focused towards that goal.

The cons

There is a downside to reading from a script when making your presentation:

- It's difficult to be passionate about a subject if you read from a script. For example: a declaration of love to your sweetheart would lose its appeal if you needed a script!
- If you read something word by word, your audience might just prefer a copy of the script so they can leave and read it (or not) at their leisure.
- A scripted delivery will be a one-sided affair, since you will not be able to include anything your audience might want to say. Sticking to a script *verbatim* automatically rules out any audience involvement.
- Reading a script minimises your opportunity for eye-contact with your audience (which, as we will see in a later chapter, will be essential).
- Using scripts requires logistical planning which may conflict with the planned style of your presentation. For example: sitting or standing behind a desk or lectern places a barrier between you and the audience – but if you remove the barriers where are you going to keep your script?
- A typical nervous response when presenting is that the hands start to shake and, if you are holding your script, this shaking will be exaggerated and more noticeable.

And

- You will have to find the time to write a script.

To script or not to script?

So, with all the pros and cons of a script, should you use one? Yes – even for relatively short presentations. Apart from the time you need to invest in writing the script, all the other disadvantages listed above only apply if you actually use it *during* your presentation and, as we have seen, there are many gains to having a script *before* you present.

If you are *given* a script, ask permission to adapt it; you will find it considerably easier to deliver if you use your own words and phrases.

The 'skeleton' framework

Start developing your script by creating a skeleton framework on a single piece of paper. Reproduced below is the starting point for the presentation shown at the end of chapter five:

The primary aim:	
The beginning	3 minutes
Signpost:	
The middle:	7½ minutes
Heading 1:	
Signpost:	
Heading 2:	
Signpost:	
Heading 3:	
Signpost:	
Heading 4:	
The end (starting with a signpost)	3 minutes
Take questions	5 minutes
Closing comment	30 seconds

You do not have to follow this exact format – find a skeleton that suits you but make sure:

- Your primary aim is reproduced at the top (to maintain your focus).
- Divide the page to reflect your chosen structure into the beginning, middle and end with sub-divisions for individual key points, signposts and any question time. Add timings for each part – you could create a separate column for this in one of the margins.
- Give each point in the middle section a heading which summarises the information you *must* communicate at each step.

ATTRIBUTES OF A MEMORABLE SCRIPT

Humour

Humour can, through laughter, involve and enliven the audience, but it can also backfire so before including humour in your presentation, ask:

- Is humour conducive to the style of my presentation, my primary aim and the expectations of my audience?
- Can I create laughter without fear of offending anyone in the audience?
- Can I really get away with telling a joke that I heard in the bar after a few drinks?

And most importantly:

Can I, as presenter, recover if the audience does **not** laugh at my humour?

Having said this, the presenter's ability to laugh at one-self can be invaluable. For instance:

🔍 EXAMPLE

Just before Harold Wilson, the then British Prime Minister, came on stage to make a speech, he noticed a button was missing off his suit jacket. So his opening line was a joke about his lack of skill in sewing and the embarrassing situations it could get him into. Had he not mentioned the missing button, the audience might have questioned his suitability to hold high office because he wouldn't notice details or because he would make a scruffy ambassador for the UK. Yet by bringing everyone's attention to it, he portrayed himself as a fallible human being who could laugh at himself – an attribute that many tend to admire.

Political correctness

The previous story and appropriateness of humour leads nicely into mentioning political correctness. For some, the world has gone too far in being 'politically correct' – but then for others it has not gone far enough.

🔍 EXAMPLE

I listened to a lady presenting a hypothetical situation about a manager who was discussing the need for improved performance with a staff member. Okay so far - until, that is, the hypothetical manager became a 'he' and the member of staff a 'she'. Since when are all managers male? Such a comment may have offended someone in the audience.

Offending a member of the audience means you run the risk of someone becoming antagonistic to you, as presenter and your presentation before you even reach the end – hardly conducive to achieving the primary aim. So, albeit that pedantic adherence to correctness can irritate (for instance, saying 'he or she' all the time): A presenter should always stay politically correct.

Positive language

The choice of words will make a substantial difference to the success of a presentation.

Q EXAMPLE

'I think it would be really great if we all make up our minds to send a man to the moon. Yes, I know it is going to be really expensive and we don't really have any idea how we are going to do it but, hey, why not give it a try? If we get him back okay who knows where we could travel to next...'

Now let's look at the actual words used by President John F. Kennedy to give the same message in his speech on 25th May 1961:

Q EXAMPLE

'I believe that this nation should commit itself to achieving the goal, before this decade is out, of landing a man on the moon and returning him safely to the earth. No single space project in this period will be more impressive to mankind or more important for the long-range exploration of space; and none will be so difficult or expensive to accomplish...'
Accepting that the speech might today fail the political correctness test (by using the terms 'man' and 'mankind'), his speech resonated with his audience to such an extent that the goal of landing on the moon, and safely returning from it, was fully realised within that decade.

So what positive words did JFK use to create such an impact? He used *believe* rather than think; *commit* rather than make-up-our minds; *accomplish* rather than try; *more impressive* and *more important* rather than really great.

The triple phrasing

Triple phrasing is another technique that can enhance the power of what is said. Shakespeare was an early exponent of this phrasing which he used in the play *Julius Caesar.*

TOP TIPS

By using positive words, a presenter will convey total belief in their message - even if they disagree with it.

> *'Friends, Romans, Countrymen, lend me your ears...'*

And Churchill used it on August 20th 1940:

> *'Never in the field of human conflict was so much owed, by so many, to so few'*

The use of 'so much', 'so many' and 'so few' has enhanced the wording substantially – look how it reads if we missed out just three words:

> *'Never in the field of human conflict was so much owed to so few'*

I suggest that the second statement has lost all the power conveyed in the original version. Triple phrasing can add power and passion to your presentation.

Stirring hearts and minds

Some presentation topics need something to create a passion, a commitment, an edge that will stir the hearts and minds of the audience. Let's take an example:

> *'There's lots of injustice and oppression in this state and I think it would be great if that wasn't the case any more.'*

So, are you stirred? Do you feel passionate about supporting the presenter in their goal? Let's try it again but with an edge this time:

> *'I have a dream that one day even the state of Mississippi, a desert state, sweltering with the heat of injustice and oppression, will be transformed into an oasis of freedom and justice.'*

You may well recognise this short extract above from the 'I have a dream' speech by Dr Martin Luther King delivered on August 28th 1963. Are you stirred now? Do you feel the passion in Dr King's words?

 **ACTION POINT**

Find a copy of Dr. King's 'I have a dream' speech. (The internet is a quick source.)
What makes that speech extraordinary? What makes those words outstanding?

Some of the key points that you should have identified are:

1. He started his presentation by quoting 'absolutes' (the American Declaration of Independence and the American Constitution). From there, everything that followed carried the authority conveyed in those documents.

2. He used facts to make his point difficult to deny. In the brief passage quoted above, he connects the heat of the desert (fact) with the heat of injustice and oppression. Yet there is no literal 'heat' in oppression – but it doesn't matter.

3. He used key themes and phrases, relying heavily on repetition: in a little over 1,500 words, he used the word 'dream' 12 times and the phrase 'I have a dream' eight times. He used 'let freedom ring' 11 times in the space of 160 words.

4. He used strong words – 'transform' rather than 'change', 'sweltering' rather than 'hot'.

5. He appealed to basic human instincts to motivate commitment. An 'oasis' in a desert is a life-saver and, by creating the link, he conveyed the message that civil rights are essential to life itself.

You may have found many more positive attributes that you could adopt to suit your own style and purpose, but do not attempt to imitate the greatest speakers the world has ever known.

TOP TIPS

Create a script by focusing on your primary aim and consider using:

- Humour
- Political correctness
- Positive language
- Triple phrasing
- How to stir hearts and minds

DRAFTING YOUR SCRIPT

You are now ready to *draft* your script preferably on a computer since it will be easier to edit if you use a computer. Upper and lower case text is easier to read than upper case alone. Using a larger than normal font size and double spacing will make it easier to read when standing to rehearse or deliver the presentation.

Place a copy of your skeleton to one side (but keep it visible) and start writing. You will need to find an approach that suits you – some start at the beginning (with 'Good morning everyone, thank you for coming...'), others prefer to write either the middle or even the ending first. It is your choice. To help:

- Refer to your skeleton framework to stay on track.
- Use your research.
- Be steered by your timings, no more than 120 words for every minute (but don't get too concerned at this stage because it has yet to be reviewed and edited).

TOP TIPS

Use punctuation! Commas will indicate a pause, full stops allow you to take a breath.

- Write your script as you would speak it.
- Don't try and finish a script at the first attempt. When you have produced a draft, give yourself a break and come back to it with a fresh 'eye'.

 **ACTION POINT**

Develop a skeleton framework for a presentation you want to make and then draft the script. Think about the appropriate use of humour, positive language, triple phrasing and stirring hearts and minds. And don't forget to stay politically correct.

An 'ABC' challenge to your draft

It is now time to challenge your draft: Is it **A**ccurate, is it **B**rief and has it **C**larity?

The challenge for **Accuracy**:
- Does it stay on track to achieve your primary aim?
- Have you accurately reflected your research?
- Have you got your facts right?

The challenge for **Brevity**:
- Have you waffled or used unnecessarily long-winded words or phrases?
- Have you (wrongly) padded the script out to fill in the available time?

The challenge for **Clarity**:
- Have you avoided jargon and terminology that your audience *might* not understand?
- Have you adhered to your chosen structure and included signposting?
- Have you written a clear message that the audience will readily understand?

 ACTION POINT

Challenge your draft presentation for accuracy, brevity and clarity, improving it as required.

TIME TO REHEARSE

You should now start a series of rehearsals of your script by speaking aloud. Check the timing – at this stage, you will probably be talking faster than ideal (we will come to the right speed later), so it will probably take you less time than that allotted. Don't forget that extra time will be needed to answer any questions.

Work towards finalising your script during your rehearsals, changing it until you are confident that it will achieve your primary aim in a memorable way.

I cannot say how many times you should rehearse a presentation, but your goal should be to feel comfortable with the content and, to an extent, *think* that you know the next line, even if you don't! As you become more familiar with your script, use a highlight pen to mark the key words or phrases. Rehearse some more, but this time only read the highlighted words and look away from the script for the rest. You will inevitably wander from the actual text, you may add a few 'ad libs', but this is fine (unless, that is, you have to deliver the script verbatim).

MOVING A SCRIPT INTO PROMPT NOTES

Assuming that you now have a final script, you can create prompts which will still give you enough information to deliver a confident, flowing presentation. Here are the main types:

• Insert **key words and phrases** into the skeleton framework. Typically these will be highlighted words used during your rehearsal.

• Create a series of **bullet points** from the key words and phrases, adding statistics, quotations etc which you have highlighted during your rehearsal. Bulleted prompts should always include the information you *must* communicate to achieve your primary aim.

- Come up with some **Presenter aids**. Sometimes, all you will need to prompt you are the visual aids that we will look at in a later chapter.
- Create **Diagrams**. A 'spider diagram' has the presentation topic in the centre of a page with lines drawn outwards to each of the key points. Link sub-points, as necessary, with further lines. Alternatively, you could develop a 'flow diagram' with a series of statements linked with arrows.

Prompts are inappropriate for verbatim delivery of a presentation, but to prevent the speaker constantly looking down at their notes, a teleprompter could be used. These project your script onto a television screen, rather like a karaoke machine. But beware the first time I used one, I veered off script. When I looked again at the screen, the operator was rolling the script backwards and forwards to try and find where I was up to. So stick to your script if you use a teleprompter!

Whichever type of prompts you choose, consider:

- Differentiating between what you must, should and could say. You might do this by using different colours or dividing your prompt sheets into columns.
- Writing notes on postcards (or card of a similar size).
- If you are using more than one piece of paper (or card) for your prompts number each page; use a new page for each key point (to stop pausing inappropriately midway through a point); write on one side only (you could lose track of whether or not to turn over); and attach the pages with loose string or a 'treasury tag' (if they fall, they won't get mixed up).
- Using a wide margin for timings and perhaps 'stage-directions'. For example: *'Display the pre-prepared flip chart'*.

Rehearse using only your prompt notes, checking that they have sufficient information.

There will always be the possibility that, when standing in front of your audience, your prompts fail to give you enough information. Don't panic! Instead:

- Always have two versions of what you intend to say – the one you are going to use and a more detailed version.
- Ensure both are at hand during your presentation.

 **ACTION POINT**

Rehearse your draft script to finalise the content, then create your prompts again. Rehearse again until you feel confident.

QUICK RECAP

- *Scripting your presentation creates a precise, consistent and complete means by which you can achieve your primary aim within the allotted time.*
- *Reading verbatim from a script can disconnect you from your audience because you won't be looking at them and it prevents you taking their comments or contributions.*
- *Create a skeleton framework for your intended script with key headings and timings before you develop it fully.*
- *Make your presentation stand out from the crowd by including, as appropriate, humour, positive language, triple phrasing and ways to stir the hearts and minds of the audience.*
- *Stay within the parameters of political correctness.*
- *Write your script as you would speak it aloud.*
- *Check a draft of your script for Accuracy, Brevity and Clarity (ABC).*
- *Rehearse your script, gradually reducing your dependency upon it, finalising its content at the same time.*
- *Devlop prompt notes from your script and rehearse again to check that they have sufficient detail.*
- *When presenting, have two versions of your script, the one you intend to use and another, fuller version, that you can refer to if needed.*

CHAPTER 8

Presenter and visual aids

'A picture is worth a thousand words'

Pictures help people to understand they tell people much more than words alone can convey – a jigsaw puzzle is much easier to complete if you have the picture of the finished result. So presenters use pictures to help achieve their primary aim, except they are no longer called pictures but 'visual aids'. I have broadened this term to 'presenter aids' to incorporate anything that can enhance your message. This is the first of two chapters on presenter aids – the second is devoted to the projection of computer images using Microsoft PowerPoint® or similar software packages.

THE ADVANTAGES OF PRESENTER AIDS

Presenter aids add value to a presentation by:

- Increasing the amount of information your audience remembers. People will absorb information by listening but will retain much more if they use more than the sense of hearing alone. There are four other senses to consider – sight, touch, smell and taste – which presenter aids can appeal to.
- Guaranteeing a more complete message is delivered, because they facilitate the audience's ability to reconnect to the presentation if they lose track.
- Fulfilling the expectations of a typical audience – few presentations are given without the use of at least one such aid.
- Acting as a series of prompts for the presenter.

Presenter aids move the focus of attention away from the presenter.

If you feel unnerved by having audiences look at you throughout a presentation, encouraging them to focus on an aid can ease some of the pressure.

Q EXAMPLE

However, aids can detract from your message and confuse the audience. I remember once sitting at a presentation which was explaining how the company was going to launch a major change in how it serviced its customer base. The audience was made up of the company's middle and senior managers (over 100 people) and the presenter, without any explanation, put up a projected photograph of a lizard. It was a great picture, close-up and in fantastic colour, but why was it there? At the end of the presentation, I asked the presenter the purpose of the picture and was told that it was a chameleon. And a chameleon changes colour according to its surroundings just as the new customer ethos would adapt to each individual customer and situation. A very clever analogy – but only if you recognise a chameleon when you see one!

CONSTRAINTS ON PRESENTER AIDS

Your choice of presenter aids will be constrained by your primary aim, by your audience, by your environment and by copyright rules.

Your primary aim and presenter aids

This is a very straightforward constraint – if an aid does not support the achievement of your primary aim, you should not use it.

Your audience and presenter aids

There are multiple constraints according to the number of people in your audience – we'll consider them in relation to the five senses:

- **Sight**: Every member of your audience should be able to clearly see the aid. For example, a flip chart will be difficult to read for anyone sitting more than five or six metres away.
- **Sound**: Whilst microphones can help the presenter to be heard by large audiences, the same cannot be said of sounds generated from computers or televisions.
- **Touch**: Handing round a demonstration model can be really effective for small groups, but it is difficult for the presenter to regain the concentration of the audience until everyone has handled it. How long would it take an audience of 50 to handle one sample?
- **Smell**: Although perhaps a relatively rare sense in presentations, you can't successfully ask an audience to enjoy the aroma of a new variety of rose, if the back row is sitting more than a few metres away.
- **Taste**: Can you realistically offer an audience of 50 a taste of a freshly baked apple pie?

TOP TIPS

You must also consider special needs when determining appropriate presenter aids. From your research, you should know whether or not everyone in your audience will gain equal benefit from introducing any particular aid.

Your environment and presenter aids

The presentation environment can constrain your choice of aid in many ways:

- Are any sight lines broken?

  Whilst supporting pillars in a room should have deterred you from using that location (assuming you had the choice), you must be certain that the audience can see you and any aid clearly. A low ceiling may not appear to be a problem, but can you raise a projector screen high enough so those at the back of the room can see over the heads of the people in front?

- Is there a reliable, usable supply of electricity at the location? One company I know were delivering a presentation abroad. They took their own technology (it was cheaper than hiring it on site) but couldn't use it because the electric current was not compatible.

- Can you control the lighting levels?

  Projected images can be difficult to see if there are other strong light sources; are there curtains or blinds you can close? A darkened room would be great for viewing projected images but a disaster for an audience who want to take notes.

- How are the acoustics?

  Remember acoustics differ when a room is full of people from when it is empty.

Copyright and presenter aids

Copyright restrictions can dramatically reduce your opportunity to use presenter aids. Here's a recent example I came across:

Q EXAMPLE

The presenter wanted to use a specific management technique that, without doubt, has a superb reputation amongst the training fraternity (and that reputation extends to those who have been trained in it). The author/creator of the technique was approached for permission, which was granted with restrictions. One of those restrictions was that the technique could not be projected onto a screen. (To be clear: the author was perfectly entitled to place as many restrictions on the use of the technique as they liked.) The presenter then had to decide whether or not the restricted use of the technique could still serve the primary aim of the presentation.

For simplicity, assume that using someone else's work as part of your presentation – be it a photograph of a chameleon, a recipe for apple pie, a management technique, a pop song or whatever, will require the permission of the originator.

CHOICE OF PRESENTER AIDS

Consider carefully which presenter aids would help you and your presentation. Your options include:

• PowerPoint® software (see next chapter)
• Flip charts
• Wipe-boards and chalkboards
• Overhead projectors
• Videos, DVDs and CDs
• A demonstration
• A 3D model
• A characterisation
• Handouts
• Microphones
• A box of tricks
• A glass of water

However, using all of the above in any one presentation will look disjointed if not chaotic!

Flip charts

Flip charts are great for recording audience feedback, drawing quick illustrations or noting key phrases.

- The height of flip chart easels can usually be altered (if not also the angle of the writing slope), although they are not always the most stable piece of equipment.
- You can pre-prepare flip charts off-site, but different easels have different methods of suspending the paper so make sure they are compatible with one another.
- The quality of the A1 writing paper varies – sometimes with cheap pads you will find the ink will 'bleed' onto the next page and that you can read the written page below a blank sheet.
- Turn onto a blank page when you are not using it. If you want to return to a specific page later, turn back the bottom corner as a marker.
- Some felt tip pens do have a habit of 'drying up' (especially if the caps are left off) so have plenty to hand.
- Check the pen colours are strong and not washed out. I would favour blue and green pens, using red for a bullet point or underlining.
- 'Normal' handwriting can be difficult to read so avoid 'joined-up' lettering.
- Some people get irritated by any spelling mistakes you make. So make sure you know how to spell any technical terms you have to use.
- You may find that the size of your lettering changes as you write and, by standing on one side of the easel, your writing may tend to slope downwards as you move across the page away from you. Faint pencil lines can help you write in a straight line. More than eight to 10 lines of text on an A1 pad will appear cluttered.
- Flip charts are ideal for small groups and perhaps medium ones.

Wipe-boards and chalkboards

Wipe and chalk boards have much in common with flip charts (although they can be more difficult to write on because they are usually fitted flush to the wall).

- Wipe-boards use non-permanent ink pens – accidental use of permanent ink is difficult to remove without a special cleaner.
- Since the requisite writing tools are 'wipe-clean', you can accidentally wipe/smudge it as you write. (And blouse and shirt sleeves are not wipe-clean!)
- Some boards have magnetic counters to quickly display posters etc.
- Others have a photo-copying facility built-in so record-keeping is easy.
- Suitable for small to medium sized audiences.

Overhead projectors [OHP]

Electronically powered, these projectors use light and mirrors to project an image from the horizontal onto a vertical (or near vertical) screen.

- These projectors have the advantage of being technically very simple (providing you know how to change a light-bulb) and relatively inexpensive to buy or hire.
- OHP images are usually pre-printed (make sure you use a large font) on A4 acetate slides.
- Beware if you are laser printing slides: *some* types of acetates have a tendency to melt in the printer! Furthermore, if you print on the wrong side of acetates, the ink will smudge.
- Using cardboard or paper frames for the acetates will help to position them squarely on the projector and provide an opportunity for you to write your prompts for each slide on the borders.
- You can write on blank acetates (with the *right* felt tip pens) to record comments or feedback from the audience, although it can look awkward if the image remains projected onto the screen throughout.

- Ensure you have space to put away the acetates you have used (they tend to slide about a little).
- Turn the projector off when changing slides.
- To keep pace with the computerisation of presenter aids, flat translucent screens linked to computers were developed to rest on the projector – but I haven't seen one used for many years.
- Suitable for small and medium size audiences.

However: OHPs have become very unfashionable – even to the point that I questioned whether I should include them in this chapter. Software such as Microsoft PowerPoint® is more widely used nowadays.

Video/DVD and CD

Whilst film and music clips can be 'dropped' into a computerised presentation, you might occasionally prefer a stand-alone television, video or CD player.

- Always cue the part of the music/film in advance.
- Know how the (remote) controls work.
- Film clips, if prolonged, can send an audience to sleep and 10 minutes can be too long in some cases!
- Check whether or not you need permissions to play any film or music clip.
- Suitable for small and medium sized audiences, assuming that they can see and hear clearly.

A Demonstration

A typical example of a demonstration would be a cookery presentation. Indeed, a successful presentation on cookery would be difficult to achieve without a demonstration, but it is not without its challenges. Your first challenge would be to get all the necessary resources arranged (ingredients, utensils, power etc). The second challenge would be to keep the presentation's momentum going whilst something is cooking – typically you would have pre-prepared the recipe up to different stages of completion. There are many variables to a cookery presentation and, in general, I would say that the more variables there are in any presentation, the greater the risk. Sightlines are vital for every member of the audience which is why televised close-ups are sometimes projected onto a screen or angled mirrors are positioned above the work area so the audience can watch the cook's progress.

A 3D Model

A 3D model (be it scaled or full size) will be essential for some presentations. For example: if launching a new car, you need to be able to show the car off; if launching a marketing campaign, you need to show the marketing materials. Although these props may be essential, again they carry risks. What if the car breaks down when being brought before the audience or a headlight fails to work? What if someone sees a spelling mistake in the printed marketing materials? Passing a prop around the audience might appeal to their sight and touch senses, but it can stilt the presenter's flow whilst the audience is still handling it. And how would you react if a so-called unbreakable prop gets destroyed by the audience?

A Characterisation

Adopting a characterisation relevant to your presentation can enliven a subject dramatically. I've seen a presenter successfully promote airline sales wearing a flying jacket and 'wired' white scarf (as if caught by the wind). Again, however, such props carry risk – might the presenter appear too flippant about their subject? I would suggest that mimicking a specific individual should not be done unless you have both the skill to carry it off and the ability not to offend – perhaps impersonating others is best left to the professionals.

Handouts

Handouts are not essential, but audiences do like them. They are a good idea:

- To ensure your audience has a copy of the *precise* message you want to communicate. This will be especially important for press releases or legal statements.
- To make good use of the time available, because you won't have to slow down for the audience to take notes.
- To convey more information/detail than your presentation time allows.
- To allow people to quote from them in the future (although this could also be a reason *not* to issue handouts).
- To allow non-attendees to read what they missed.
- When the room layout excludes a writing surface for the audience.

Having thoroughly proof-read the handouts, you must then decide when to distribute them:

- Before your presentation.
  This gives people time to read and think about the subject and therefore encourages questions and discussion. However, don't assume they will have read them, nor should you assume that they will bring them to the presentation – so take some spares.
- At the start of the presentation.
  This helps people to make any additional notes and listen more attentively. However, people tend to read (or skim-read) ahead, which can be very distracting for the presenter.
- During a presentation.
  This is not recommended unless the handouts directly relate to a stage in your presentation when you want the audience to break from listening – perhaps to start a discussion. It will disrupt your flow as presenter and it may be difficult for the audience to 'settle down' again.
- After the presentation.
  Do tell the audience at the beginning of your presentation that you are going to distribute handouts at the end and how comprehensive they are. The audience can then decide whether or not to make additional notes.

Assuming that everyone has an email address, you could take a greener perspective and email the handouts to the audience before or after the presentation.

Microphones

We will talk in a later chapter about 'projecting' your voice, but large audiences and/or large rooms often warrant the use of a microphone. Even if you test whether or not your voice can carry to the back of an empty room, when it is full of people sound will get absorbed more readily – and shouting is not an option! Should you decide on a microphone be it static, hand-held, clip-on (to your clothes) or as a headset:

- Do a sound-check when the room is empty.
- Be aware that some microphones require you to also carry a transmitter. When choosing your clothes, make sure you are wearing something that can accommodate it – a belt, for instance.
- Know either how to turn it off or, if controlled by a sound engineer, how to signal them when you want it turned off. The last thing you want is to leave the stage area and be caught saying things you would rather the audience didn't hear!
- Hold a microphone so that you talk 'over' rather than 'into' it.

A box of tricks

You are in the middle of your presentation and someone needs writing paper, another wants a pen, your felt tip pens dry up and you have just tripped on a cable that is dangerously stretching across from a power point. Forethought can help you overcome many of these potential risks by having 'a box of tricks'. The content of my box includes:

- Writing paper
- Pens
- Pencils
- Pencil sharpener
- Erasers

- Permanent ink marker pens
- Wipe-board pens and cleaning pads
- Ruler
- Masking tape
- Scissors
- Stapler and staples
- An extension lead
- A calculator

And it doesn't end there: I also carry cough sweets, sticking plasters, headache pills, tissues, all just in case. I will not run the risk of losing my voice, nor suffering from a headache minutes before I start.

A glass of water

This is an incredibly valuable presenter aid and the one that I would recommend you should *always* have. Apart from easing a dry throat (a typical response to nerves), it is invaluable when you need to take a moment or two to gather your thoughts – perhaps after a difficult question or when you fear losing your way. A sip of water will often help you to re-gain focus.

PRESENTER AIDS AND RISK

Felt tip pens dry up, projector bulbs burn out, computers crash. Be prepared – *anything* could happen! If you doubt your ability to quickly rectify any equipment problems, consider having on-site back-up available. Always set up your presenter aids before the audience arrives and test that it is all as you expect.

> The most important risk to manage must always be the Health and Safety of the audience and yourself.

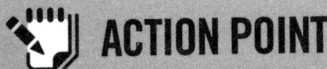 **ACTION POINT**

Choose a presentation that you have to deliver and identify three presenter aids you could use to support your primary aim. Why have you chosen these three?

 QUICK RECAP

- *Only introduce presenter aids if they serve the achievement of your primary aim and beware of using too many aids in any single presentation.*
- *Presenter aids include using PowerPoint® software, flip charts, wipe-boards, chalkboards, overhead projectors, videos, DVDs, CDs, demonstrations, 3D models, characterisations, handouts, microphones, a box of tricks and a glass of water.*
- *Aids add value by enlivening a presentation and (if used effectively) will increase the retention of information by your audience.*
- *The inappropriate use of presenter aids can distract if not confuse the audience.*
- *Environmental constraints could reduce your choice of presenter aids, as will the size and make up of the audience*
- *Before using any materials originated or produced by others, ensure that you have the necessary permissions.*
- *Always manage the potential risks which may arise when introducing a presenter aid, especially Health and Safety issues for you and your audience.*

CHAPTER 9

PowerPoint®

Vacuum cleaners were invented in the middle of the 19th century, but it wasn't until the early part of the 20th century that a man called Boss Hoover produced his first electrical carpet cleaner. He didn't design it – Murray Spangler did – but today the term Hoover® has become generic for different makes of vacuum cleaners across the world. Such is the professionalism and popularity of the Microsoft software package PowerPoint®, that it is also becoming (if it has not already become) a generic term for any software package that generates images for screen projection.

PowerPoint® software has become widespread and it is *the* professional presenter aid available to most presenters, which is why it warrants a chapter of its own.

AN INTRODUCTION TO POWERPOINT®

For fear of making assumptions about your existing knowledge or comfort level with technology, let's start with the basics:

- You will need a 'host' computer with a presentation software package which you can use to write your presentation.
- Your presentation is developed by typing and inserting content onto a series of slides (like the pages of a book).
- Unless you can take the host computer with you to the location of your presentation, you will need a second computer to deliver it.
- At the location, you will need a projector to transfer the images from the computer onto a screen that can be seen by everyone in the audience.
- When you present the slides, a click of the mouse is just one of the ways you can turn the pages as your presentation unfolds.

Simple! Or maybe not...

EARLY CHALLENGES

Before starting to write your presentation, check the following points.

Is it appropriate to the size of your audience?

PowerPoint® works exceptionally well for audiences of a medium or large size but would be somewhat over-the-top for just one, two or even three people. Too often, it becomes the 'default' of presenter aids and may not always be necessary. Ask yourself whether or not it genuinely adds value to your presentation and the achievement of its primary aim.

Is the software compatible?

If you will be using two computers (one to prepare, one to deliver) check that they carry the same software packages and note that different versions of the same software package *might* inhibit the functionality.

Can you transfer material between computers?

Using two computers will mean that you need to be able to transfer the written presentation from one to the other – some computers are security programmed to prevent you from saving a file onto a portable device.

Will you have access?

A second computer might be password protected – will you be able to access it? Will the computer used for the presentation 'talk' to the projector? I once hired both a computer and projector from the same company to avoid this risk, but it still didn't work!

Do you know how to operate it?

Projectors may be built-in at a location. Do you know how to work the controls?

Do you know which cables connect to which sockets if you are taking your host computer? I recently delivered a presentation to a group of IT specialists at their location. I had used the location before without difficulty and assumed – wrongly – that should I have any unforeseen technical challenges, they would be the people able to help. The room's technical console was so complicated that it took three people over 30 minutes to get everything connected properly. Thankfully, I had arrived very early!

And finally

Think about the cautionary tales we have already explored about both the location and general use of presenter aids: Will you have electricity? Will everyone in the audience be able to see the screen?

And most importantly, ask:

Will the use of PowerPoint® slides support your primary aim?

USING POWERPOINT®

What should a slide look like?

Start with a template which will determine a series of key elements for every slide in your presentation including:

- The background – do you want a single colour or perhaps a graphic of some kind over which the typeface can appear?
- Would borders enhance the appearance of the slides?
- Should anything appear on every slide, such as a copyright notice or a corporate logo?
- Do you want to number each slide?
- What font type, size and colour would you like? Bold or italic? Upper case should only be used, if at all, for headings. As a guide, 10 or 12 lines of text should be the limit per slide, which suggests a font size of no less than 20. Seek to standardise the font size across all the slides in a presentation.
- How will any bullet and sub-bullet points look?
- Do you want to 'animate' the presentation?

TOP TIPS

PowerPoint® software has pre-developed templates which not only save you time but also achieve a coordinated appearance across the different elements. You can adjust the elements in each template but do so with caution; you don't want to end up with white lettering on a white background!

When determining your template consider:

- Landscape slides are preferable to portrait ones – not least because most screens are wider than they are high.
- Do you need or want to reflect your corporate standards? This might include the choice of font, colours and how to use the logo (for example, some logos cannot be used in close proximity to anything else, others must be shown with a predetermined ratio of height to width).

- If presenting to another company, do you want to use their corporate style? Think about any restrictions there might be – including copyright.
- If using both your audience's logo and your own, consider the relative size: do you really want yours to be larger than theirs?
- Are there any subliminal messages you could incorporate? For instance, different shapes sub-consciously send key messages. My corporate style uses red triangular bullet points because, I was told, they say 'dynamism' – I can't honestly tell you whether or not it is true!
- Is the lighting level in the room going to wash-out the projected images? If so a dark background (such as dark blue) with light coloured lettering (yellow or white) will work best.
- Don't over-do the styling – it is the message that you type on the slide that is important and you do not want to detract from it with textured backgrounds, background pictures etc.
- Are you going to print the presentation, perhaps as handouts? Dark backgrounds can use a lot of ink!

Albeit in black and white, here's a reproduction of my 'standard' template:

Heading – size 44, bold, maroon, centred

▲ The style of the slides reflects my company's corporate identity

▲ All text is in black using Garamond, minimum size of 24, left margin

▲ The bullet points and border are maroon (picking up on one of the colours in my corporate logo)

▲ This template includes a copyright statement (but in font size 8) and my company's logo.

© Executive Shadows Ltd 2009

Developing your slides

You can now use your template to develop your presentation. Some guidelines:

- Create an introductory slide with the title of your presentation and your name.
- Avoid the appearance of a disjointed presentation by creating a sequence of slides for the entire presentation rather than an odd slide here and there.
- As part of your introduction, consider showing the key points that you will be talking about in the middle part of your presentation. As you complete each point in the middle section, you can reproduce this same slide as a signpost that you have finished one point and are moving on to the next.
- Bullet points are much easier to read than prose.
- Generally, the content of each slide should only be what you **must** communicate to your audience. The absence of more information will allow you, as presenter, to have more to say than what the audience can read for themselves.
- The meaning of abbreviations and acronyms should be clear from reading the slides. For example: A heading might say 'The ABC of Presenter Aids' and the text will identify that this refers to Accuracy, Brevity and Clarity.
- Using clipart will enliven your presentation, but only if it is relevant (remember the chameleon!).
- Scanning and then reproducing forms (for instance, a tax return) on a slide does not work well because people will try (and often fail) to read them.
- Diagrams, pie-charts etc are much better than columns of figures.
- If you want to show a website, it may be safer to reproduce the pages than risk a 'live' connection that could fail or be too slow. Don't forget copyright issues as well.
- You can 'drop in' film clips.

- Finish with a closing slide, perhaps with thanks to the audience for their attention.
- Proof-read the slides carefully.

So for a 20 minute presentation, it is likely that you will have, at most, the following nine or 10 slides:

- Welcome, presentation title and your name.
- Your primary aim.
- Your headings for the middle.
- A slide expanding each of the three or four key headings of the middle section.
- A repeat of the slide with the headings (to show you have covered them all).
- Any questions.
- Thank you and, as appropriate, your contact details.

Sound and sound-effects

If showing a film clip, check that the equipment can achieve sound levels that the back-row of the audience can clearly hear. I am not a fan of introducing sound-effects like a ricocheting bullet to accompany the clip art of a gun being fired or a round of applause to signal the end of your presentation – but it is your choice.

Animating your presentation

You can 'build' slides with a basic level of animation where they 'develop' in front of the audience. So when a slide first appears, it might contain only the heading and perhaps some clip art. Each time the mouse is clicked, a bullet point will appear. (The keyboard or a remote control can be used to achieve the same result.) This has the distinct advantage of preventing the audience from reading ahead whilst you are still talking about the first bullet point. You will need to introduce a means, however, by which you will know when there are no more bullet points to animate on any particular slide:

TOP TIPS

Put a full stop after the last bullet point on each slide – you will then know that, on the next mouse click, it will move onto the next slide.

You can programme the slides to move on (to the next bullet or next slide) automatically at a set time, perhaps at three second intervals. This will only really work successfully if you plan not to talk at the same time since the audience will be distracted by the visual and stop listening to you.

There are multiple ways that slides can be animated. For example it can also be used to emphasise or indicate that you are moving on to the next point (by removing, shrinking, fading etc). You can also animate the way that each slide follows another. It can be great fun to experiment with all the different ways that you can animate your presentation, look at any tutorial your software provides or check the internet for ideas. However, never use more than two types of animation within your presentation – it can irritate if not confuse the audience.

DELIVERING YOUR PRESENTATION

TOP TIPS

Check in advance that your presentation will not be interrupted by a screen-saver, a pre-timed scan of the computer or the projector moving into stand-by mode.

Open your presentation before the audience arrives to avoid looking unprofessional. If your presentation is going to be immediately followed by another, consider merging the two presentations into one file, or use a function key to 'blank' the projected image (but will retain the image on the computer allowing you to open the second presentation).

You can also briefly stop the presentation by 'blanking' both the projected image and the computer screen. For example, with my keyboard I press the letter 'B' and the screen goes blank until I press another button.

Projected images might appear on the screen wider at the top than the bottom (known as the keyhole effect). To manage this, the simple trick is to angle the top of the screen forward or, for the technically minded, most projectors allow you to adjust the image to create the landscape shape reproduced on your computer screen.

You should face the audience and, tempting as it will be, avoid looking at the projected images when presenting. It is for this reason I dislike (intensely) the use of pointers (be they manual or electronic) – they force you to look at the screen and away from your audience.

To look at the audience, you should, therefore, have a computer screen in front of where you will typically stand and, by glancing down, you can see where you are up to in the presentation. Built-in projector systems often have a lectern with an inset computer screen which at least allows you to stand behind it – but a lectern is a barrier between you and the audience and therefore shows a potential lack of confidence on your behalf.

You can, with some computers, over-write by hand on top of pre-developed visuals, perhaps to highlight or underline text. You can also use it to record audience feedback directly onto a blank slide just as you would use a flip chart. This has the added functionality of giving you the option to transform your handwriting into text, saving it and emailing it to the attendees before they return to their desks.

Printing options

PowerPoint® software gives you a number of ways to print your presentation which can be very useful for the audience and/or the presenter. They include:

• Handouts with space for people to add their own notes.
• Adding a script or prompts on the same page as each slide.
• Printing multiple slides on one page to give you an overview of the entire presentation.

Advancing technology

Such is the speed by which technology and software advances, I cannot hope to be up-to-the-minute in advising you of the full capabilities available to you. Check out online tutorials to pick up tips on the full range of features available to you. Whatever software is available to you, learn how to use it and perhaps most importantly:

Rehearse, rehearse and then rehearse some more!

 ACTION POINT

Assuming that you can gain access to a computer with presentation software on it:

Develop PowerPoint® slides (or equivalent) to support you in successfully delivering a presentation. Create the following slides:

1 An introduction
2 Your primary aim
3 Your key headings for the middle section
4 A guide for further content under eacgh heading in the middle
5 A summary slide (which might repeat the primary aim slide)
6 A closing slide

Then animate the slides and practice the presentation.

QUICK RECAP

- *Computer generated images projected onto a screen are a highly professional way to support you when presenting to medium and large groups.*
- *PowerPoint® software is just one of a range of software options, although it is perhaps the best known.*
- *Check (as with using any presenter aid) that it supports your primary aim and that the technology will work at your location.*
- *Careful planning and forethought can eliminate or reduce the likelihood of any risks to using technology.*
- *Use a template for your slides, be it developed from scratch or pre-formatted in the software options.*
- *Create a sequence of slides which will progress from the start to finish of your presentation.*
- *Use bullet points to state the information that you must communicate to your audience and enliven the slides with clipart, diagrams, pie-charts etc.*
- *Sound effects are likely to distract the audience but if you do need to use sound, check in advance that all the audience will be able to hear.*
- *Introducing animation, especially to 'build' the content of a slide, is keenly encouraged providing that the number of different animation techniques is restricted.*
- *Check if your computer enables you to over-write content onto slides.*
- *Look at the audience, not the screen, when delivering your presentation.*
- *Make use, as appropriate, of the various printing options available to you.*
- *Explore what your technology can do for you – its capabilities and applications are evolving at a rapid pace.*
- *Rehearse your presentation thoroughly.*

CHAPTER 10

Questions and answers

So far in this book we have looked at presentations as something of a one-sided affair – the presenter does all the preparation, all the talking and all the 'doing'. And it may be tempting for you to do just that and leave the stage. However, effective communication should be two-sided by including some form of participation. Therefore the least a presenter should do is to include a question-and-answer element, which is the subject of this chapter. In the next chapter, we will look at other forms of participation to create a successful presentation.

QUESTIONS

Asking questions

As presenter, you can ask the audience questions. Some presenters feel that this will settle their nerves if their audience participates at an early stage. You might use questions to check the audience's existing knowledge levels (against your research) or to give people a reason to listen to the presentation.

'Hands up anyone who has used flip charts in a presentation before.'

'Is anyone concerned about how they can handle difficult questions when giving a presentation?'

You have to be careful when asking your audience a question. If we look carefully at the first question above, whatever answer you get, it won't really impact the presentation you are about to make. However, if we asked the second question at the start of a presentation and everyone indicated that they have no concerns, the entire purpose of a presentation could collapse. Pre-script your questions to have exactly the right wording, so that whatever answer you receive, it will not negate what is about to follow.

Now, compare the following two presenter questions – which do you prefer?

What is the subject of your next presentation, John?' and
'Susan, what is the subject of your next presentation?'

The second question is infinitely better than the first. Using Susan's name at the beginning will ensure that she will listen carefully to the question – John might have been daydreaming and wasn't aware that you were speaking to him until it was too late. Thus, John might be embarrassed and it would now be likely that he, if not more of the audience –will feel negative towards you and your presentation.

 **ACTION POINT**

Think about a presentation that you are going to make.
Script three questions you can ask the audience that, irrespective
of the answers, will not disrupt your flow or the achievement of your
primary aim.

Taking questions

There is a distinct advantage to taking questions throughout your
presentation – not least because if the audience do not understand,
they will stop listening unless they can interrupt (with a question)
and seek clarification. The disadvantage to this approach, however,
is that you can lose your place in the script, give information out
of sequence and lose track of your timing.

The safer option (for the presenter) is to take questions at a
specified point in the end section of your presentation. This avoids
the disadvantages above, but inevitably runs the risk that the
audience might 'lose the plot' at some point and stop listening.
So if you take this option, say at the start that you would like
questions at the end, although should they require clarification, it
is okay to interrupt.

On very few occasions, however, questions may be inappropriate – perhaps when making a speech or when you make a
statement about an on-going legal situation. However:

If you refuse to take any questions, the audience will either
believe that you have something to hide or that you are running
scared.

ANSWERS

Preparing your answers

It may sound strange to think about how you will answer a question before it is even asked, but as part of your preparation you should think about the questions your audience is likely to ask and collate any information that you will need to respond effectively (if not have additional presenter aids prepared). Having said that, you shouldn't plan to deliver an incomplete presentation; answers to the most likely questions should have been addressed in the presentation itself.

In reality, it is unlikely that you will think of all the questions you might be asked. If you adopted the method in chapter two of sorting information into the three categories of what must, should and could be communicated, the answers to most questions will often be found within the 'could' communicate category.

Answering questions

There are some principal rules when answering questions:

- Put your notes/script aside – you don't want to give the impression that you have prepared answers.
- Listen carefully: don't interrupt.
- If you don't understand the question, ask for clarification.
- Pause (briefly) before you answer – it conveys thoughtfulness.
- Be succinct in your answer but give some new or additional information to encourage further questions.
- Avoid entering into a dialogue with the questioner.
- Don't suggest that the questioner should have listened closer to your presentation.
- Without being pedantic in response to every question, thank them for the question and check that you have answered it to their satisfaction.
- If you know your questioner, don't drop your guard or become flippant – they deserve a reasoned answer like everyone else.

Generally, the audience will expect and want more than a one word answer to a question, yet a straightforward 'yes' or 'no' can be a very powerful response. You can follow it up with your reasoning if appropriate.

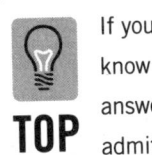

TOP TIPS

If you don't know the answer, admit it.

Dangerous questions

If your first instinct is to wonder about the significance, relevance or naiveté of a question, be wary. In all probability, there will be a follow-up question or series of questions which will take you and your audience totally off track. Before answering, ask the questioner for a more specific question, perhaps giving it a context or by giving an example. For example:

> *'In respect of how to handle difficult questions, you have asked me to agree that it is better to refuse to take any questions at all. Could you give me the scenario you are thinking about when that might be appropriate?'*

Potentially, some questions may be designed to entrap you into a position that reverses in whole or part the position you took in your presentation. For example:

> *'Would you agree that it is important when presenting to convey absolute belief in your message?'*

Answer: 'Yes'

> *'And that should be the case even if you personally doubt the integrity of what you have to say?'*

Answer: 'Yes'

> *'So on the basis of your answers, is it not more than possible that you have, albeit very convincingly, just told us all a pack of lies?'*

Another type of entrapment can be generated by hypothetical questions:

'Hypothetically, what if I made a presentation to, say, a group of medical experts and they asked me a question about...'

Whatever the rest of this question may or may not be, it is not hypothetical. The questioner is thinking about a specific situation but failing to give you all of the information. In such circumstances, you could ask for more information (which may or may not be forthcoming) or, taking a safer route, say:

'I would need to have some more information to give a correct response to your question, please come and talk it through with me after the presentation has finished.'

And if the questioner resists your deferment, you can add something along these lines: *'I know that some people are a little pressed for time and I don't want to overrun and cause them to be late home. Please come and see me at the end.'*

Multiple questions can confuse both you and the audience and often are a means to wrestle control of the presentation away from you:

'Why shouldn't we make a stab at answering all questions even if we don't know the correct answer, because isn't it important to gain the respect of the audience in trying to answer and why are you giving us all these danger signals when people like me ask perfectly reasonable questions: or are you going to avoid answering me?'

In response, you should note each question (or ask someone else to do it for you) and, repeating each in turn, provide the answer.

Dangerous questioners

Some questioners may adopt an aggressive and/or negative attitude when asking a question. They deserve an answer and should receive one. Stay calm, do not adopt a similar attitude. To avoid the audience becoming negative, you need to counterbalance that attitude, for example:

'You have every right to your own opinion, but I would re-iterate that the principles I have outlined about answering questions have been tried, tested and proven by a multitude of presenters over many years. Not only would I not presume to place my opinion above such a weight of expertise, but my own experience bears out that such principles are perfectly sound.'

Some questioners have so many questions that no-one else can get a word in! Without care, the end result will be a conversation between you and this one questioner, with the rest of the audience rapidly losing interest. Repeating a question to the whole audience means that you offer your answer to them rather than an individual. Then, avoid eye contact with the persistent questioner **immediately after** you have answered their question. If their questioning still persists, ask whether anyone else in the audience has any questions. If the questioner *still* persists, say:

'You obviously have some really good questions to ask and I suspect I haven't yet given you all the answers. Perhaps you could stay back at the end and we can talk through any of your additional questions then. Thank you.'

If you can't think of an answer

It's flattering to the questioner for you to pause before you answer – it says that it is a good, thought-provoking question. But what if you can't think of the answer? There are a number of 'tricks' you can try:

- Repeat the question: *'So I have just been asked what you can do if the answer doesn't occur to you?'* This buys you time to think and you may find that the answer now springs to mind. If that doesn't work...
- Take a sip of water. The mouth can feel dry when in a stressful situation (having everyone look at you struggling to find an answer is often stressful) and the water can not only alleviate the dryness but again buy you time. But if that doesn't work...

- Ask the audience. This is a frequent trick used by trainers when they don't know the answer to a question. They ask for other people's views (and, on occasion, the questioner's personal view) to stimulate their own thinking. Then, the trainer sums up or comments on the views expressed by the audience before adding any personal thoughts that have occurred. But if that doesn't work either...
- Admit you don't know. (Sometimes it is better to admit you don't know at the outset.) However, when you admit you don't know, commit to finding out and giving them the answer within a set time-frame. Ask them if the time-frame is acceptable to them; when you get their agreement to this, you will have appeared to have successfully dealt with the question. Be seen to make a note of the question and don't forget to ask them to leave their contact details with you.

If you don't get any questions

You might find that when you offer to take questions, no-one says anything. To give people a little time to switch from listening mode to talking, give an advance signal of your intention:

'In a few moments, I will invite you to ask any questions that you might have, but just before I do that I would like to say...'

If you still haven't been asked any questions, try one of these openers:

'A question I was asked just before I started was...' or
'The most frequently asked question I get on this subject is...'

You can make up the question and providing you give them some new or additional information, it will usually encourage others to start asking questions. And there's another use of this technique:

TOP TIPS

Asking a question of yourself enables you to introduce information that you might have forgotten to mention during the presentation itself.

CLOSING QUESTION TIME

In your planning you should have allotted a maximum period of time for taking questions. If it appears that you have taken the last question, but still have time remaining, ask something like:

'Are there any other questions that anyone can think of?'

Having counted silently to six, if there are still no more questions:

'That's fine. If you do think of any, please contact me at....'

(Have a pre-prepared visual available with your contact details.)

You should always have a positive closing statement worked out to finish with. This ensures that no matter how tough the questions have been, your presentation will end positively.

Always have the last word after questions to end on a high.

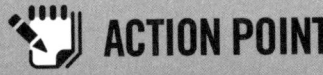

ACTION POINT

Using the same presentation topic as the earlier exercise, think of the three worst possible questions you could be asked. How would you answer them?

QUICK RECAP

- *Audience participation in a presentation will enhance (if planned correctly) their understanding and make it a memorable event.*
- *Pre-script any questions which you, as presenter, intend to ask of the audience.*
- *Questions from the audience should be encouraged, but it is up to you to choose when to take them.*
- *Be wary of questions which might seek to entrap you into saying something that you do not intend.*
- *Never adopt a questioner's negative or aggressive attitude.*
- *You should pre-prepare answers to likely questions.*
- *In answering questions be succinct and try to give some new information. If you don't know the answer, admit it.*
- *End a question and answer session with a positive statement.*

CHAPTER 11

Audience participation

You can read and memorise all the available books and advice on how to drive a car, but it is only by interacting with an instructor (and a car itself!) that you can really begin to understand and learn how to drive – it's the same with a presentation. An interaction between the presenter and their audience will enhance understanding and make your presentation memorable. The type of participation you could introduce will vary according to the size of your audience and what you have learnt from them through research. Your options include: the presenter asking questions; the audience asking questions; using an icebreaker; facilitating a discussion; involving the audience in something practical.

This chapter will now explore ways to include audience participation over and above question and answer sessions and consider your response to uninvited audience participation.

ICEBREAKERS

These are techniques which, at the start of a presentation, are designed to informally bring everyone together, concentrate their minds and/or energise the audience.

For a large or medium sized audience:

• You could simply ask the audience to introduce themselves to two or three people sitting nearby and shake hands – this is particularly good when people don't know each other.

• You could divide the audience into smaller groups and ask them to write three bullet points on a flip chart – be it three things they have in common, three key reasons for attending etc. Follow it with a brief review (be it by a member of each group or you as presenter).

• A more fun icebreaker could be to energise the audience with some form of activity – perhaps mild aerobics/stretching exercises. Don't forget to accommodate anyone with special needs that your research identified.

For smaller groups:

• You could ask people to briefly introduce themselves to the rest of the audience. You will need to brief them as to what information you would like – perhaps their name, company, role and the reason(s) why they are there. Each person can then either introduce themselves or the person next to them.

• You could achieve the same result in a more creative way by asking people to draw a picture of themselves at work on a large piece of paper. Then ask each person to explain their drawing.

• Just asking people to arrange their seating by order of their birthdays or the street number of their house (flat or whatever) can also break the ice successfully.

There are a myriad of possible icebreakers – be inventive but do not use anything that disrespects either your audience or the seriousness of your presentation. Also, think about what will work for the specific audience that have been invited to your presentation by considering their number, whether or not they know each other and any special needs that they may have. Note, not all presentation topics will be suited to using an icebreaker.

 **ACTION POINT**

Identify three ways that you could break the ice at the start of a presentation on a topic chosen by you. Which would be best and why?

DISCUSSION GROUPS

You could deliver your presentation and then move into a discussion. Before starting the discussion, brief the audience on the purpose of the discussion and decide your precise role:

- Are you going to 'chair' the discussion?
  This will require you to take notes and then summarise the outcome (perhaps with intermediate summaries, especially if the discussion is going off track). You will also have to ensure that it achieves the declared purpose within the allotted time. As 'chair', you should not express your own opinion.
- Are you going to participate in the discussion?
  If so, you will need to have pre-arranged for someone else to take on the role of chair described above. You should also sit amongst the audience rather than at the front to show that you have, temporarily, relinquished control.

If you introduce a discussion session into your presentation, you must accept the outcome – even if you disagree with it.

If you want a discussion amongst a large audience, you could sub-divide it into smaller groups. Each group wider be required to feedback their conclusions to the wider audience. You should not use this approach, however, if you seek a consensus amongst the audience (because you will probably have diverse results from the different groups).

When the discussion is finished and the outcome summarised, you as presenter should re-take control and draw the overall event to a positive conclusion.

PRACTICAL INVOLVEMENT

As mentioned in the chapter on presenter aids, you could give people a 3D prop to 'play' with, investigate or review.

Trainers and facilitators often use custom-made business games to drive a message home. A simple alternative is to adapt a child's activity for example:

Q EXAMPLE

Give teams 10 minutes to build as many paper aeroplanes as possible to a prescribed standard. One team will declare itself the winner almost immediately because they have the most planes, but the elimination of planes not meeting standard will almost always result in the 'winner' being another team. The intended messages, therefore, are that it takes time to deliver quality and poor quality wastes resources (in this case, paper). Such messages are far more likely to be remembered and applied effectively than if the presenter just told people 'produce lots but don't waste resources'.

You could conclude your presentation with a quiz to check the audience's understanding, providing they have a strong chance of success if they are to take a positive message away from your presentation. It is safer for an audience to answer quizzes in groups rather than as individuals.

UNINVITED PARTICIPATION

Let's not forget that the audience might decide to participate when you least expect it. Preferably this might be to applaud, cheer or laugh – providing it is in the right places! Accept such accolade gratefully and don't try to continue your presentation until things calm down.

You may, however, have *unwelcome* participation which can include the following:

 **ACTION POINT**

Having already looked at possible icebreakers for your presentation, now consider whether or not you can include some form of participation (in addition to questions) that would serve your primary aim.

Unexpected laughter

It is difficult to advise you what to do in these circumstances since you may well be unaware of what the audience is finding so funny. Here's a genuine example:

Q EXAMPLE

I (yes, I admit it) once formed a group into teams and gave each team a name. The teams couldn't stop laughing and it took me some time to find out the cause. Little did I realise that one of the given names had an alternative, very crude, meaning in New Zealand (where, it happens, one of the attendees had lived).

If you challenge the audience's laughter, it may be they don't want to embarrass you or are simply too embarrassed to admit what is so funny – it might not have anything to do with you. If laughter is prolonged, my best advice is to arrange an adjournment and ask a trusted member of the audience what was so funny.

The audience talking/whispering amongst themselves

Stop talking and wait – the silence alone will usually encourage people to pay attention and, if not, looking directly at the 'culprits' should do the trick. If the talking continues, you could ask if they have something that they wish to share with the rest of the audience – but we are moving here into a rather strict 'schoolteacher' mode and that can cause your audience to turn against you and your presentation. Should two culprits persist, you could change *everyone's* seating arrangements when they return from a break. (See the icebreakers above.)

Heckling

Some politicians love being heckled because it brings out their best – but many others will hate me for saying this! I have seen very different responses to hecklers. To totally ignore them and continue with the presentation becomes a battle between the loudest voice and yet stopping the presentation until they finish (if they do finish, that is) is giving them exactly what they want – your audience's attention. So what can you do in response to hecklers?

Responding with a smile can work and a succinct line can also work well:

> *'I know I am hitting the mark with my comments when someone decides to heckle me...'*

I have seen presenters verbally attack hecklers for poor manners or their lack of magnetism in securing an audience of their own, but I haven't seen this work successfully without a follow-up eviction from the room (an option not open to many types of presentations).

Crucially, never engage with a heckler and address any response you do decide to give to the audience. Above all, stay calm.

🔍 EXAMPLE

One successful tactic I have seen is where the presenter catches the gist of the heckled message and then responds along the lines of:

'Someone in the audience wants to know what I think about (for instance) capital punishment. Well I'll tell you if you'll listen...'

And when the heckler persisted:

'You will have your turn to speak as much as you want later – after I have finished. I'm sure the audience will stay on to listen to any valid point that you feel needs to be made...'

QUICK RECAP

- *Audience participation in a presentation (if planned correctly) will enhance understanding and make it a memorable event.*
- *Participation can be achieved with icebreakers, group discussions and/or some form of practical involvement.*
- *Participation can be both unintended and unwelcome, although a skilful approach should enable the presenter to turn it into an opportunity.*

CHAPTER 12

The presenter's voice

Have you ever been midway through watching a film on television and increased the volume so you wouldn't miss anything or fail to understand the film's plot?

Alas audiences don't have the same control over the presenter's voice. They can ask the presenter to speak louder, but the odds are that five minutes later the presenter's voice has dropped back to its starting position and that is when the audience stops even trying to listen. This chapter focuses on finding the 'right' voice as a presenter and that isn't just a question of volume, there is much more to consider as we will see (and hear!).

Special note: For you to get the most from this chapter, you will need to read some of the text aloud. You may want to be alone!

EMPHASIS, STRESS AND TONE

We're going to start with an exercise:

ACTION POINT

There are six people in a room, Arthur, Betty, Chris, Dawn, Eddie and Fiona. Arthur has just told the group that he believes one of them has stolen his wallet. In turn, each person says: 'I didn't steal your wallet.'
What might Arthur have learnt from each person in the group? Note down your answers.

Now, read aloud each of the following five statements putting *strong emphasis* **only** on the words shown in bold:

* '**I** didn't steal your wallet' said Betty
* 'I **didn't** steal your wallet' said Chris
* 'I didn't **steal** your wallet' said Dawn
* 'I didn't steal **your** wallet' said Eddie
* 'I didn't steal your **wallet**' said Fiona

Now let's look at what we can understand from these five 'speeches':

* Betty stressed the word **I** which, by implication says that she may well know who did steal Arthur's wallet.
* Chris protests innocence by emphasising **didn't** (perhaps too strongly, rather like a child who tries to avert responsibility when they are clearly to blame).
* Dawn has implied that rather than **steal** the wallet, she merely borrowed it.
* Eddie stressed that he didn't steal **your** wallet, but maybe he has stolen everyone else's!
* Fiona has emphasised **wallet** but she might still have stolen all the contents.

It may be that by studying the tone of voice, we can only identify one total innocent, Betty – and she may well know who actually stole the wallet. So:

> The tone of voice you adopt can totally change the meaning of key words and phrases.

ACCENTS

We all have an accent of one type or another. Great, accents add 'colour' and, unless particularly broad, you should not try to diminish it as a presenter. In determining whether or not your accent is too 'broad' for your audience, think about how often people have asked you to repeat what you have just said. If it has happened frequently, especially with people living in the area where your audience are based, you *may* need to moderate your accent.

Are you (like me) prone to pick-up or mimic the accents of the people around you? I now live on the South Coast of England, but whenever I go back to my 'roots' in the North, my accent changes. This is perfectly natural and we do it, often sub-consciously, to 'belong' to the new circle of people we are with. Whilst adopting the 'local' accent can be good because you are building a relationship, a rapport with your audience. It could be that you cause offence by, in the eyes of the audience, having some 'fun' at their expense. The safest option has to be sticking to your own accent rather than imitating another.

MELODY

Your voice should have melody, and avoid being a monotone. Your accent will typically have this melody 'built-in', which is another reason to retain it. Do not take this to extremes, it is not a singing competition, but speaking your words at slightly different pitches will make it easier for the audience to listen.

Presenters have a tendency to forget, when speaking, that they need to breathe – the longer the sentence, the less power your voice has to deliver it and it tends to drop away so the audience doesn't hear the ending.

 ACTION POINT

To demonstrate how your voice loses its power, read aloud the sentence above (shown in italics) without pausing or stopping (in other words, ignore all the punctuation).

Did your voice waver towards the end? Let's try it again:

Read aloud the same sentence but this time, deliberately raise the pitch of the last few words.

If you were successful here, well done! If it was difficult let's add a little more guidance:

Read aloud the same sentence, but this time use the punctuation to briefly pause (and breathe) *and* deliberately raise the pitch of the last few words.

Anyone listening to that last exercise should have heard every word you said, even the last few.

A melody will only be successfully achieved if you breathe and a successful melody will not only avoid a monotonous delivery but it will help your audience to hear everything that you say.

PRONUNCIATION AND PACE

The quicker that you speak, the more likely it will be that your pronunciation will falter:

ACTION POINT

Read aloud the following *as quickly as you can*:

'She sells sea shells by the sea shore and the shells she sells are surely sea shells.

Since she sells shells by the sea shore, I'm sure the shells she sells are seashore shells.'

Did you stumble on any of the words? Did any of the words merge into one another? If so:

Read aloud the passage again, but this time at a speed where your pronunciation of *each* word can be clearly heard.

Adopting a slower pace of speaking than your 'normal' speed will automatically improve your pronunciation. However, to be certain that each of your words is clearly spoken, you may have to listen to a recording of your voice. Alliteration (the repetition of a sound or letter) in the tongue-twister above should be avoided in presentations – why make things more difficult for yourself?

 TOP TIPS

The sections in chapter two on what you must, should and could communicate and in chapter five on signposting are essential to identify your 'right' presenter voice. You may find it useful to re-read those sections before the rest of this chapter.

VARYING YOUR SPEED

You need the audience to not only listen to what you say but also to understand it. Therefore you have to find a balance between talking too slowly (potentially creating boredom and impatience amongst your audience) and racing to the finish. Equally, however, talking at the same pace throughout a presentation is almost as bad as adopting a monotonous tone – so how do you find a balance?

Imagine yourself driving a car. You start off in first gear and as things progress you move up a gear and then another. As you arrive at junctions and signposts, you drop your speed and move down a gear before picking up the pace again. As you arrive at your destination, you gradually slow down again until you have reached a full stop.

And it's the same with the speed of your presentation, albeit you will only use three speeds (or gears).

- **The beginning section of your presentation:**
  Start at a slow pace, in first gear. People need to get used to the sound of your voice and they will find it easier if you speak slowly. *Gradually* pick up the pace into second gear, slowing down to first gear again when you reach the end of the beginning and the first signpost.

- **The middle section:**
  Say the first heading in first gear (which is what you **must** communicate), move into second gear for what you **should** communicate and if you include anything that you **could** say, you will be in third gear (because it doesn't overly matter if the audience remembers that part). You will slow down into first gear for the next signpost and heading before speeding up again – and so on until you reach the end of the middle section.

- **The end section:**
  Starting in first gear, you are unlikely to advance beyond second gear in this section.

As you develop this technique, you should achieve a smooth change between the gears, just as a proficient car driver would.

 **ACTION POINT**

Practise three speeds of talking by reading aloud either a script that you have prepared or a copy of a speech you can find on the internet.

VOLUME

You should now have practised a presenter voice with clear pronunciation with variations in melody and speed. Now, we need to make sure that it is heard by projecting your voice to the back of the room. So:

- Keep your chin up (looking down at notes will suppress the power of your voice).
- Look at the audience, if you must turn away from them, stop talking.
- Talk to an imaginary person *behind* those furthest away from you and if you speak loud enough for that imaginary person to hear, so will others.
- Do not shout – the 'voice' you should use is akin to coaxing a child or a dog to come to you from some distance, without fear of being chastised.
- Speak louder for what you **must** communicate and adopt a slightly softer voice for what you **could** communicate.
- If you have a relatively high pitch to your voice, you will need to drop that pitch to successfully raise the volume.

SILENCE IS POWER

Silence can be a very powerful way of communicating. Assuming that you have punctuated your script, you have already identified when a pause is required – if only to tell you to take a breath!

A pause can also say 'I have just made an important point, and before I move on to the next, think about it!'

Despite its power, silence can be unnerving for presenters who then add speech fillers like 'um', 'er' and 'you know' to fill any gaps – albeit subconsciously. To manage these superfluous sounds:

- Count silently to yourself when introducing a pause – one, two and three, and re-start.
- Take a sip of water (the best presenter aid you could ever have).
- Slow down your speed of talking.
  And
- Stop thinking about it! The more you think about *not* saying 'um' (or whatever), the more you *will* say it.

 ACTION POINT

Practise your presenter voice which will incorporate a melody, clear pronunciation and a varying speed and volume.
Remember to use silence as appropriate, and to breathe!

And don't forget: in your research, you should have identified anyone with special hearing needs and you must respond accordingly.

QUICK RECAP

- *Your own accent, unless particularly broad, can be an asset not a liability when presenting.*
- *When speaking, remember to breathe!*
- *Pronunciation must be clear and will be helped if you avoid alliteration in your script.*
- *Varying the pitch, speed and volume of your voice is important – not least to reflect the information that you must, should and could communicate.*
- *Silence can be powerful, especially to give emphasis to the preceding words.*
- *Do not forget to accommodate any special hearing needs.*

CHAPTER 13

Using your stage and body language

You suspect that someone close to you has just told you a lie, and you want the truth. So you ask them to repeat it but this time they have to 'look you in the eye'. What does looking into their eyes 'tell' you that their words and voice cannot? Body language – and the eyes are just one part of this huge subject – can reveal what you are *really* thinking irrespective of what you are saying. Your instincts, your conscious and sub-conscious mind will tell you whether or not a speaker is sincere, is confident and, perhaps above all, being honest but we are generally rather poor at seeing ourselves as other people do. This chapter seeks to help you to avoid sending 'bad' signals to others and also advises you how to look sincere, confident and honest – even when you are not.

UNDERSTANDING BODY LANGUAGE

Before reading about body language let's try a simple exercise to demonstrate how much you already understand about body language.

 ACTION POINT

Watch *without sound* a television 'soap' or drama. (This exercise will produce better results if you choose one that you do not normally watch.) Record it at the same time.

With a notebook and pen, note down specific body language that you believe each character is sending to another in the programme. Is their body language positive or negative?

At the same time, note down what you think is the gist of the different story lines you are watching.

Play back the recording, this time with sound. How accurate were your observations?

On the basis that understanding body language is largely instinctive and that it can form a substantial part of any communication, an anticipated outcome from the exercise will be that you achieved some success in:

• Correctly recognising many positive and negative signals.
• Correctly understanding much of what happened during the programme

Although you may have correctly recognised the positive and negative body language in the exercise, be wary of misinterpretation. There are different ways that the same body language could be interpreted. For instance, if you sit with your arms folded, it could mean:

• You are withdrawn, even submissive
• You are comfortable
• You are cold

Nevertheless, should a presenter fold their arms, it will not give a good impression. The audience doesn't particularly want you to be comfortable (it will appear casual rather than comfortable). They wouldn't be interested in you being cold (unless they were also cold and hoped you would turn the heat on) and they certainly don't expect you to be withdrawn. Folding your arms would not, therefore, give a good impression.

CULTURE, PROFESSIONS AND BODY LANGUAGE

The perceived meaning of body language changes across different cultures and even between different professions. For example:
- To walk into a room late would be offensive in some cultures but in others, reflects the seniority of the last person to arrive.
- People have 'personal space' that they prefer you do not encroach upon.

Q EXAMPLE

When seeking to demonstrate this idea of 'personal space' on a training workshop, two people were asked to walk towards each other and stop when they no longer felt comfortable. They ended up practically touching! No personal space there then. Whilst considering how I might de-brief this without asking whether or not there was any sexual chemistry between them, I discovered that one was a dentist and the other a dental nurse. In their profession, they had to be comfortable with invading each other's (and their patient's) personal space.

It's important to bear these alternative cultural and professional meanings in mind when considering the role of body language in presenting.

The following recommendations on body language reflect the *predominant* interpretation attributed to them in the UK but such will differ across cultures and professions.

TOP TIPS

As a presenter, you need to do everything possible to make a positive first impression on your audience, who will make their mind up about you and the presentation within a matter of seconds, even before you have started speaking. So you must get it right. Plan in advance:

■ Your appearance
■ Your 'staging'
■ Your entrance

INFLUENCING BODY LANGUAGE

Your appearance

There are a few obvious things to start with here:

• You should be 'well-groomed'.

• Are your clothes comfortable? Do not wear brand new clothes at a presentation – you don't know whether or not the buttons and zips are reliable! New shoes sometimes 'squeak' so wear what you know.

• Do not distract the audience with your appearance. For instance: jewellery can catch the light, be noisy or move about too much (such as a loose, sparkling bracelet) and avoid clothes with printed wording or 'cartoons' (someone will try to read then).

• Ensure your appearance is 'fit for the purpose'. You may need to move about the stage, bend down, twist around: will your clothes and hairstyle stay in place?

Having said this, how smart should you be? Well, if you are too smart (or too scruffy), you could make some of the audience uncomfortable so think in advance about how the audience is likely to dress. A guide:

Wear clothes a little smarter than the audience to show respect for them and they are more likely then respect you and your presentation.

Your staging

The area from which you are going to make your presentation is referred to as your 'stage' (even though it may not be a raised dais) and you should endeavour, whenever possible, to have it arranged before your audience arrives. If you are following on from a previous presenter and have to reset the stage in front of the audience, do it quickly and calmly before you start speaking. Here's a proposed layout:

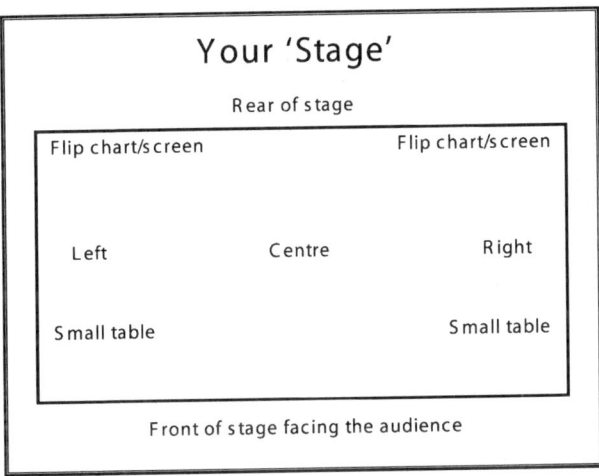

A few general observations:
- To avoid standing in front of (and therefore blocking) a projected image on a screen, it is preferable to position the screen to one side.
- Unless you are using it throughout the presentation, place the flip chart to one side, only bringing it to centre stage when needed. If you are right-handed, stand with the easel to your left – you will find it easier to write on.

- A small table set to one side is ideal for your notes, a computer (if required) and the recommended glass of water.
- You will be delivering the bulk of your presentation from the centre of the stage, now clearly marked, and will be able to glance down at your notes and/or computer without having to move.
- If you add a chair, desk or lectern, they should be placed centre stage. However, as discussed earlier, lecterns and desks both represent a defensive barrier behind which it can appear as if the presenter is 'hiding'.
- A chair can be placed at the side of the stage and brought to the centre to use if and when appropriate – perhaps when taking questions or chairing a discussion.

TOP TIPS

Start 'on your feet' even if you choose to sit down later. Sitting down throughout a presentation is only recommended for small groups since it lessens the degree of control you have over an audience.

Guidelines on using the stage

- The 'front and centre' of the stage should be used at the start and end of your presentation.
- The centre is where you should spend most of your time, but moving from side to side promotes interest and therefore improves the audience's attention.
- Step forward (from the centre) to the front of your stage when you emphasise a point – what you **must** communicate. (This could be simultaneous with the louder, slower voice that was discussed in the last chapter.)
- Step to the left or right of the stage when you want the audience to participate.
- Standing at the rear of the stage is saying 'I'm not doing anything right now'. Use it when you want the audience

to concentrate on a visual aid or when they are working on something (at your request) without your involvement.

- Don't stand between the audience and the visual aids.
- Never invade the 'personal space' of your audience. If you are standing and they are sitting, you really need to be at least a couple of metres away.
- Remember that as long as you stay 'on-stage' some of the audience will look at you. If you don't want that, leave the stage.

Your entrance

How you walk on to your stage is crucial – you must exude confidence and calmness (however you might feel inside) yet avoid the potential for arrogance. Walk to the centre of the stage in a curve rather than a straight line. When you stop, it says 'I have arrived', and will avoid signalling that you would rather keep walking in a straight line right out of the room!. Avoid shouting over any chatter to gain attention – your stage 'presence' should be enough to do this.

MAINTAINING A POSITIVE IMPRESSION

Your body language while presenting

Your body language should support your spoken words. So if you are seeking to convince the audience on a certain point, adopting hesitant, withdrawn body language will destroy any impact that your words are designed to achieve.

You should aim for body language that is relaxed but confident.

If the words are a song and your voice the music, then your body language is the dance. Those that can deliver these three elements in harmony have mastered the art of communicating a message.

TOP TIPS

There is one golden rule on body language: always be yourself and be natural. Trying to emulate the body language of a speaker you admire will look false.

Whilst the danger of misinterpreting body language has already been mentioned, you can, with a fair degree of certainty, give a positive impression if you:

- Face your audience – your shoulders (and body) should be parallel to the front row of seats.
- Smile. It says 'I'm glad to be here' and relaxes the audience, placing them more firmly 'on the side' of your presentation and primary aim. Don't smile if you are delivering bad news.
- Make eye contact with your audience: especially when making an important point or when challenged by the audience. You should seek to make eye contact with as many people in the audience as possible during your presentation, avoiding the natural inclination to make eye contact only with your friends. Break off eye contact before it becomes a stare.
- Avoid any tendency to slouch.
- Take deliberate (rather than small or half-hearted) steps. At other times, keep your feet on the ground. Don't balance on one leg, rock on your heels, or raise your toes off the floor.
- Keep your hands away from your neck, head or hair: it is at best distracting and at worst a sign of nervousness if not lying.
- Use 'open' hand gestures: by showing the palms, rather than the back, of your hands. Don't fidget! If you lose 'control' of your hands, put one hand in a pocket for a little while, but to retain your composure, ensure that your thumb is outside of the pocket or only your thumb is inside. Make sure you have empty pockets (except, perhaps, for a handkerchief).
- Value your prompts. If you throw them aside when you have

finished talking, you are inviting the audience to do the same with their notes.

- Keep your elbows away from your body – I don't mean look like a chicken flapping its wings, just allow the audience to see a small gap between your body and your elbows. It will give you a confident, relaxed appearance.
- Avoid sudden movements. Whilst your body language should not be too over-the-top, it should be somewhat more exaggerated that 'normal'.

If I itch, do I scratch?

Yes, within reason! Trying to ignore it could distract you and potentially cause you to lose track of where you are. If you scratch an itch (briefly), it's gone and your audience will probably not even notice, but there are some itches that discretion would say ignore!

Bad habits

Rehearsing your presentation in front of a video camera (or, failing that, a mirror) can reveal mannerisms and habits that you are totally unaware of.

Q EXAMPLE

When I filmed James making a presentation, he clenched one fist and slapped it repeatedly into the other when asking for questions from the audience. It was only when he saw the film-clip that he realised why no-one dared ask him any questions!

However, it is too easy to watch oneself on film and say 'I did that wrong, and that, and that and...' creating an endless list of mistakes. Remember that the purpose of rehearsing is just as much about saying what's good, what's 'in-the-bag' as recognising what can be improved. Seeking others' observations is often a more balanced way to get both the good and not-so-good perspective.

You must rehearse your presentation and, be it with help or by your own assessment, learn how you can create a positive impression by adopting the right body language.

 **ACTION POINT**

Ask one or two colleagues whom you trust to watch you rehearse a presentation and give you feedback as to your positive and not-so-positive body language.

QUICK RECAP

• *Body language is a significant part of communicating an effective message.*

• *Interpreting body language is not exact – the same signal can mean different things depending on cultural and professional interpretations.*

• *First impressions count – make sure you give the impression you want.*

• *Think carefully about your appearance.*

• *Ensure that, whenever possible, your 'stage' is laid out as you wish before the audience arrives and then use it to good effect.*

• *Standing gives the presenter greater control than sitting, but the former may be inappropriate for small groups.*

• *Learn positive body language signals to support your message.*

• *Securing feedback on your body language during a presentation from people you trust can be a very effective way to learn.*

CHAPTER 14

Dealing with nerves and setting positive goals

Nerves are perhaps the greatest hurdle to overcome for most presenters. Yet it is when a presenter takes the stage *without* nerves that it is most likely to go wrong because nerves are, in fact, a good thing – they will make you do your very best and avoid a blasé attitude creeping in. But you do have to manage nerves, so that they help rather than hinder you in making a successful presentation. In this chapter we'll look at different ways as to how you can do this.

MANAGING YOUR NERVES THROUGH PREPARATION

Thorough preparation is essential to manage your nerves and that preparation includes:

- Setting a *realistic* primary aim describing what you want to achieve with quantifiable goals so you can *objectively* review your success.
- Conducting thorough research so that you know your subject and your audience.
- Doing your utmost to ensure that your location is right for your presentation.
- Determining and then sticking to a structure for your presentation.
- Developing a script and appropriate prompt notes.
- Supporting your primary aim with appropriate presenter aids.
- Developing the 'right' voice and body language.
- Rehearsing and then rehearsing some more.

In short, everything we've covered so far in this book could be said to work towards managing your nerves, but there is yet more you can do, including:

- Adopting quick solutions to common nervous reactions.
- Setting yourself a personal goal, your secondary aim.
- Using positive affirmations.
- Pre-stage self-management.
- Creating belief.

MANAGING NERVOUS REACTIONS

Quick solutions to common nervous reactions

When I ask a group of presenters for the possible nervous reactions which they have experienced, it is typically a long list. Here are some of their most common thoughts:

You will forget to say something

You are the only person in the room who knows that you have forgotten to say something so move on. If it really is that important, start your question-time by saying *'A question that I have been asked before on this subject is...'* and then ask the question which will allow you, in the answer, to pass on the missed information.

Your mind goes 'blank'

It happens to the best of us! That's why you have your prompts and back up script. If they don't work – maybe because you can't remember where you are up to – deliberately go back in your script to a part that you know you have said and start by saying: *'To recap what we have said so far then.'* Taking a sip of water can also help you to re-focus.

You lose your place in your script

This does happen when you stop using your script for a while and then suddenly realise you need to refer to it again – but you can't find where you are up to. To avoid it, even if you aren't really using the script, make sure that you turn the pages as you talk and, if you have highlighted key words and phrases in your script, you should be able to find your place quite easily.

Blushing or sweating

What to do when your cheeks or neck redden... First, tell yourself that the audience will not be as aware of it as you are. Second, if you think this might happen, ensure that the room temperature is cooler than normal. Third, consider asking the audience a question. Not only will that divert attention away from you (which should help) but it will also distract you because you will have to concentrate on your answers. If you are prone to sweat, wear light-coloured tops and high collars can cover some of a reddening neck.

You feel sick before starting

The taste in your mouth is a reaction to stress and a drink, sweets or gum can often work – but make sure you aren't eating when you take the stage.

You feel dizzy

Ever heard people say take three deep breaths? The irony of this is that we don't usually use our full lung capacity – until, that is, we take deep breaths. I have found that the surge of air, ie of oxygen, can actually make me feel dizzy, so it is something I would avoid. Instead, I would sit down quietly, steady my breathing pattern and take a sip of water. You could also try one of the multitude of relaxation techniques available.

Your body starts to shake

Move the body part, whether it's your hands or knees. Frequently this can happen when you are trying to over-control your body language – a bit like trying to hold still a cup and saucer and finding that the more you try to be still, the harder it is.

Your notes get mixed up

This shouldn't happen if you have only written on one side of your notes and you have loosely tied them together. If you do get lost try checking the page numbers or your highlighted key phrases to find your place.

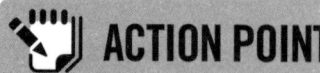 **ACTION POINT**

If you think you will feel nervous about making a presentation in the future, consider how you might react.

What strategies can you put in place, before you present, to manage these reactions?

Now you have thought about how you will manage your nerves, you can take this to the next stage by setting yourself a realistic goal for your forthcoming performance.

Setting a personal, secondary aim

In chapter one, we set a primary aim for your presentation, declaring to your audience what would be achieved as a result. We also referred to a non-public aim – a secondary aim – which would describe what you want to achieve personally. Again, this aim needs to have multiple measures and, as far as possible, be objective. For example:

During this presentation, I will demonstrate my improved skills which will be evidenced by:

1. Having my stage area and presenter aids set up before the audience arrives.
2. Smiling as I walk, in a curve, onto my stage.
3. Sticking to my allotted time.
4. Communicating everything that I **must** say.
5. No-one asking me during the presentation to 'speak-up'.
6. Not clenching my fists at any time.
7. Being asked at least three questions by my audience.
8. Remembering to thank the audience for their attention when I finish.
9. Receiving a round of applause at the end.
10. At least one person complimenting me when the presentation is over.

Having 10 measures of success has a distinct advantage in that should I fail in one, perhaps forgetting to smile, I will still have been 90% successful. However, this list is only illustrative since it is very ambitious – especially for an early attempt at presenting. As humans, we can only do so many conscious things at the same time.

🔍 EXAMPLE

One Christmas, I was given a drum kit and couldn't master (all at once) the reading of music, the right foot doing one thing and the left another, the left hand playing the snare drum and the right the cymbal (or was it the other way around?). Since I couldn't consciously learn to do everything at once and, being a not-so-patient teenager, I gave up. Don't fall into this trap. Be patient with yourself and don't give up.

Create a list of all the things that you want to improve

- Learn each skill one at a time until it becomes a sub-conscious activity, then move on to the next.
- When you reach the end of the list of things to learn, start a new list. Never stop learning and refreshing your skills or they won't be there when you really need them.
- If you try to do everything right on the first attempt, it is likely that you will fail on all counts.

Use positive affirmations

The purpose of affirmations is to deliberately change the way that you are thinking. Let's first look at the mindset of a nervous presenter:

TOP TIPS

Rehearse, rehearse and rehearse again until much of what you do on your 'stage' is sub-conscious.

'This is going to be a disaster. I'll break out into a sweat, drop my notes on the floor and forget everything I was going to say'

It will not be too surprising if our nervous presenter then went onto the stage and started sweating, dropped their notes and forgot everything! It's as if they talked themselves into it – and in a way that's exactly what has happened. Have you ever said that something was bound to go wrong? It then did go wrong and all you said was 'I told you so!' It's almost as if you didn't want to be proved wrong if things had gone right!

Positive affirmations work in just the same way but with a positive outlook. Let's try again:

'I will be calm and confident throughout this presentation.'
'This presentation is going to be really successful.'
'I am going to make a brilliant presentation.'
'I will enjoy making this presentation.'

You will only need one or two affirmations (too many could confuse you and diminish their impact) and watching yourself when saying them can add to the positive influence they can have:

TOP TIPS

Repeat positive affirmations aloud three times whilst looking into a mirror with a smile on your face!

Be careful how affirmations are worded – they should not be negatively based. For example, avoid: 'I will *not* drop my notes on the floor' or 'I am *not* going to panic'.

Sources for your affirmations could be generated by:

• Thinking how you will feel when your presentation reaches its successful conclusion.
• Your list of things you want to do differently when presenting.
• Positive feedback that you received in the past.
• Thinking about what your friends and family would say in support of you.
• Asking the people requesting you to make the presentation why they chose you. This might give you some positive comments such as *'you always present so professionally'* or *'you know more about it than anyone else'*.

TOP TIPS

Use any feedback you receive as a way to identify your strengths as well as your weaknesses

ACTION POINT

Write down three positive affirmations that you will use as part of the preparation for your next presentation. Practise saying them to yourself in a mirror.

Pre-stage self management

Q EXAMPLE

I was minutes away from starting a two day training session on presentation skills when one of the attendees asked me if he could leave! If ever my positive affirmations were going to be challenged, this was the time. It certainly wasn't the sort of message that I needed minutes before I started. What was I supposed to say? How was I supposed to start in that confident, calm, smiling way that I have been advocating? So I asked him why he was asking for my permission. His reply was that his boss had said he could leave if I agreed. It wasn't getting any better – so I asked again. It transpired that he had recently attended another such event on making presentations and thought mine would therefore waste his time. Thanks very much! I convinced him to stay until the first break and, if he didn't learn anything new, he was free to leave. Whilst he ended up staying for the full two days, it was definitely not the best start to my day.

The 10 or 15 minutes *before* you take the stage are crucial minutes in which you should prepare yourself mentally to deliver a great presentation.

You will need to experiment until you find the best routine that works for you before you take the stage. It might include:

• Repeating your positive affirmations.
• Talking to lots of people or no-one at all.
• Being in a noisy or a very quiet space.

- Having a drink (no alcohol naturally).
- Reviewing your notes (although be careful – it's a bit like last-minute cramming for an exam and you could convince yourself that you have forgotten everything).
- Going to the toilet.

ACTION POINT

What are you going to do to remain calm and confident in the 10 to 15 minutes before your next presentation starts? Make a list and check it is realistic given your location, timing etc.

You must:

- **Believe and create belief in your message.**

  Be particularly careful when you don't whole-heartedly agree or support the message you have to present, since you could place the achievement of your primary aim at great risk. Such uncertainty could be hinted at by an inappropriate word or phrase, your tone of voice betraying your negative feelings or poor body language (such as refusing to make eye contact at key points).

- **Believe in your audience.**

  Believe that they want to hear you, believe that they want to get something out of your presentation and believe that they are 'on your side'. Seeing your audience as an ally will make it a lot easier than seeing them as an enemy or a group of intimidators.

- **Believe that you can do this.**

  Use positive affirmations and self-management of time before you start your presentation.

Belief evidences itself by the presenter being credible, trustworthy, positive, enthusiastic and passionate about their subject.

And, if all else fails, remember:

> Whatever you feel like internally, the trick for success is to exude positive belief externally.

QUICK RECAP

- *Nerves are a good thing when presenting – they will help you to perform at your best.*
- *Thorough preparation (looking at each element within this book) is the foundation of a successful presentation.*
- *Know how you might react when nervous and then develop a strategy to minimise the effects.*
- *Set yourself a realistic personal aim which will objectively measure your success as a presenter.*
- *Don't try to develop your presentation skills 'en masse', work on different aspects until they each become an automatic, sub-conscious skill.*
- *Use positive affirmations to convince yourself that you will be a successful presenter.*
- *When given feedback about a presentation, listen carefully for the good as well as the not-so-good.*
- *Identify what you should do in the 10 to 15 minutes before you start presenting to ensure you are in a positive state of mind – and will remain so.*
- *Believe in your message, your audience and yourself.*

SUMMARY OF KEY POINTS

1. SETTING A GOAL FOR YOUR PRESENTATION

- Define the primary aim of your presentation: what is your presentation seeking to achieve?
- Identify multiple ways to measure the success of a presentation.
- Remember there are three types of presentations: to give information, facilitate a discussion or stimulate action. Identify which type you are going to make to clarify your primary aim.
- Ensure that you will know at the end of a presentation that the audience have understood what you intended to convey. Understanding is one of the main measures of success for a presentation.
- Apply five tests to your presentation's primary aim to determine whether or not it is: agreed by others; realistic in its ambition; the right medium; worthwhile; and to be delivered by the right person, you!
- Use your primary aim to focus your attention during the preparation and delivery of your presentation.

2. RESEARCHING AND SIFTING CONTENT

- A balance must be achieved between giving the right amount of information for your audience to absorb and still managing to achieve your primary aim.
- Before you start researching, determine how you will organise the information you gather.
- When embarking on research, forget everything that you think you know about the subject.
- Good research will find contradicting information. This is healthy; it helps you to make your own mind up about issues.
- The information you gather during your research may well be subject to copyright restrictions. Make sure you check.
- Seek out as many possible sources of information as possible.

- When you have investigated all other sources of information, add your own knowledge and experience.
- Classifying information into different types (eg facts) will help to ensure that you will use the information to best effect.
- Once you have become familiar with the research, consider putting it to one side whilst you develop your presentation.
- Categorise the information into what you **must, should** and **could** communicate to achieve your primary aim.
- Before signing off on the work you have undertaken, validate that you have adhered to the principles we have outlined about the amount of information and your research for your presentation and you will achieve your primary aim.

3. YOUR AUDIENCE

- Publish your primary aim to your audience whenever feasible and check that it will meet their expectations – *before* you start your preparation.
- If the subject of your presentation must remain confidential until the last minute, seek to manage the rumour and speculation that will occur.
- Invite not only those who are needed to support your primary aim but also those who might challenge it. Invite advocates of your primary aim who have the power and/or influence to counteract any negativity.
- Pro-actively accommodate any special needs the audience may have.
- Invitations to your presentation should offer incentives for individuals to attend (as well as stating the time, place etc).
- The more you know about your audience and their attitude towards your primary aim, the better you will be able to hone your message and, therefore, achieve success.
- Pitch the content of your presentation above the average

knowledge level of the audience yet never assume they will understand terminology and jargon.

* Adapt the experiences of other successful presenters to suit your own style but don't try to mimic someone else's style.

4. LOGISTICS AND THE LOCATION

* Logistics need detailed planning, but never assume that your plans will work perfectly.
* Locations should be chosen by balancing convenience (for the audience) and the overall cost-effectiveness.
* Your primary aim will have a direct impact on determining the appropriate layout of the room, which in turn will dictate the size of room required.
* Your audience should be made comfortable, but not too comfortable. Think about the type of seating and whether or not tables are desirable.
* Develop the staging area to enable rapport building, not least by ensuring that the presenter and visual aids can be seen and heard by every member of the audience.
* Be prepared to manage unwanted distractions and interruptions.
* Seek to achieve the right levels of temperature and lighting.
* Always pay attention to special needs and Health and Safety requirements.
* Don't restrict your planning to just the room for your presentation, consider other areas that you and your audience will need to use.
* Create a timetable from the moment that the room becomes available until it has to be cleared.
* Communicate your logistical needs in writing and make sure you receive confirmation in writing.

- Recruiting on-site logistical help can be invaluable to respond to unforeseen problems.
- If your primary aim cannot be achieved in the location, for whatever reason, either change the location or scale down what you planned to achieve.

5. CREATING A STRUCTURE

- Remember that the audience will not be listening to every word, so you need to make it easy for them to 'reconnect' with your presentation with a clear structure and signposts.
- Thorough research is an essential step to creating a structure.
- All structures have a beginning, middle and end. In each part, there is information that you must, should or could communicate.
- A straightforward approach to structuring a presentation is to have a logical sequence of key points of roughly equal duration, but not too many to cause information overload.
- Divide the available time for your presentation amongst the points you wish to make, and those you should or could make.
- Close on a highly positive statement.

6. A MORE CREATIVE APPROACH TO STRUCTURE

- Whatever structure you adopt, make sure you stay on track with your primary aim.
- All presentations should have some form of structure including a beginning, middle and end along with appropriate signposting.
- Having lots of multiple points within the middle section of your presentation can increase the possibility that your audience will become confused.
- Combining too many different structures in the same presentation is exceptionally difficult and not to be recommended.

7. SCRIPTS, PROMPTS AND MAKING IT MEMORABLE

- Scripting your presentation creates a precise, consistent and complete means by which you can achieve your primary aim within the allotted time.
- Reading verbatim from a script can disconnect you from your audience because you won't be looking at them and it prevents you from taking their comments or contributions.
- Create a skeleton framework for your intended script with key headings and timings before you develop it fully.
- Make your presentation stand out from the crowd by including, as appropriate, humour, positive language, triple phrasing and ways to stir the hearts and minds of the audience.
- Stay within the parameters of political correctness.
- Write your script as you would speak it aloud.
- Check a draft of your script for Accuracy, Brevity and Clarity (ABC).
- Rehearse your script, gradually reducing your dependency upon it, analysing its content at the same time.
- Develop prompt notes from your script and rehearse again to check that they have sufficient detail.
- When presenting, have two versions of your script, the one you intend to use and another, fuller version, that you can refer to if needed.

8. PRESENTER AND VISUAL AIDS

- Only introduce presenter aids if they serve the achievement of your primary aim and beware of using too many aids in any single presentation.
- Presenter aids include using PowerPoint® software, flip charts, wipe-boards, chalkboards, overhead projectors, videos, DVDs,

CDs, demonstrations, 3D models, characterisations, handouts, microphones, a box of tricks and a glass of water.

- Aids add value by enlivening a presentation and (if used effectively) will increase the retention of information by your audience.

- The inappropriate use of presenter aids can distract if not confuse the audience.

- Environmental constraints could reduce your choice of presenter aids, as will the size and make up of the audience.

- Before using any materials originated or produced by others, ensure that you have the necessary permissions.

- Always manage the potential risks which may arise when introducing a presenter aid, especially Health and Safety issues for you and your audience.

9. POWERPOINT® SOFTWARE

- Computer generated images projected onto a screen are a highly professional way to support you when presenting to medium and large groups.

- PowerPoint® software is just one of a range of software options, although perhaps the best known.

- Check (as with using any presenter aid) that it supports your primary aim and that the technology will work at your location.

- Careful planning and forethought can eliminate or reduce the likelihood of any risks to using technology.

- Use a template for your slides, whether it's developed from scratch or pre-formatted in the software options.

- Create a sequence of slides which will progress from the start to finish of your presentation.

- Use bullet points to state the information that you must communicate to your audience and enliven the slides with clipart, diagrams, pie-charts etc.

- Sound effects are likely to distract the audience but if you do need to use sound, check in advance that all of the audience will be able to hear.
- Introducing animation, especially to 'build' the content of a slide, is keenly encouraged providing that the number of different animation techniques is restricted.
- Your computer might enable you to over-write content onto slides; check if this is the case in advance.
- Look at the audience, not the screen, when delivering your presentation.
- Make use, as appropriate, of the various printing options available to you.
- Explore what your technology can do for you – its capabilities and applications are evolving at a rapid pace.
- Rehearse your presentation thoroughly.

10. QUESTIONS AND ANSWERS

- Audience participation in a presentation will enhance (if planned correctly) understanding and make it a memorable event.
- Pre-script any questions which you, as presenter, intend to ask of the audience.
- Questions from the audience should be encouraged, but you should choose when to take them.
- Be wary of questions which might seek to entrap you into saying something that you do not intend.
- Never adopt a questioner's negative or aggressive attitude.
- You should pre-prepare answers to likely questions.
- In answering questions be succinct and try to give some new information. If you don't know the answer, admit it.
- End a question and answer session with a positive statement.

11. AUDIENCE PARTICIPATION

- Audience participation in a presentation will enhance (if planned correctly) understanding and make it a memorable event.
- Participation can be achieved with icebreakers, group discussions and/or some form of practical involvement.
- Participation can be both unintended and unwelcome although a skilful approach should enable the presenter to turn it into an opportunity.

12. THE PRESENTER'S VOICE

- Your own accent, unless particularly broad, can be an asset not a liability when presenting.
- When speaking, remember to breathe!
- Pronunciation must be clear and will be helped if you avoid alliteration in your script.
- Varying the pitch, speed and volume of your voice is important – not least to reflect the information that you must, should and could communicate.
- Silence can be powerful, especially to give emphasis to the preceding words.
- Do not forget to accommodate any special hearing needs.

13. USING YOUR STAGE AND BODY LANGUAGE

- Body language is a significant part of communicating an effective message.
- Interpreting body language is not exact; the same signal can mean different things depending on cultural and professional interpretations.
- Different cultures have different interpretations of body language.

- First impressions count. Make sure you give the impression you want.
- Think carefully about your appearance.
- Ensure that, whenever possible, your 'stage' is laid out as you wish before the audience arrives and then use it to good effect.
- Standing gives the presenter greater control than sitting, but the former may be inappropriate for small groups.
- Learn positive body language signals to support your message.
- Securing feedback on your body language during a presentation from people you trust can be a very effective way to learn.

14. DEALING WITH NERVES AND SETTING POSITIVE GOALS

- Nerves are a good thing when presenting – they will help you to perform at your best.
- Thorough preparation (looking at each element within this book) is the foundation of a successful presentation.
- Know how you might react when nervous and then develop a strategy to minimise the effects. Set yourself a realistic personal aim which will objectively measure your success as a presenter.
- Don't try to develop your presentation skills 'en masse', work on different aspects until they each become an automatic, sub-conscious skill.
- Use positive affirmations to convince yourself that you will be a successful presenter.
- When given feedback about a presentation, listen carefully for the good as well as the not-so-good.
- Identify what you should do in the 10 to 15 minutes before you start presenting to ensure you are in a positive state of mind – and will remain so.
- Believe in your message, your audience and yourself.

TROUBLESHOOTING QUESTIONS

What if I am never given enough forewarning to develop a script?

If you know that, at some point, you will be asked to make a presentation on a given topic, then prepare it in advance. For example: every time there is a new or updated product, the sales manager should write at least a 'prompt' card as to the key benefits of the product. This card should be part of a library of cards that are constantly updated, so whenever a presentation on their products is requested, they can simply extract the relevant prompts.

However, if you are asked to present on a subject for which you cannot do any advance preparation, you have two choices – agree a low-expectancy primary aim or refuse to present on the basis that you will not be able to achieve the required outcome (what would be the point?).

What if the technology fails?

Your planning should have minimised this possibility, but it can still happen. If you have arranged for on-site backup, you could call for help whilst your audience has an unscheduled break. Alternatively, you could talk through your pre-prepared handouts.

Should none of the above resolve the situation, briefly apologise (but only once – don't repeatedly refer to the lack of technology) and go ahead without the aids. You might also change the format of the presentation so there is more participation (perhaps a discussion) which should take some of the pressure away from you.

What if I totally disagree with the message and doubt that I can be convincing?

Short of refusing to do the presentation, start by researching the background to the subject and why the message needs to be delivered. You may find that once you understand it, you also agree with it. Assuming that you still disagree, look for the parts of the message you do believe in and devise a structure to deliver those first, thus reducing the proportion of the message with which you have to be particularly careful.

One approach is to script the opposite message (the one you do believe in). Rehearse this briefly until you achieve the right (that is, supportive) voice and body language. Then, insert the few words it will take to reverse the message. For example: 'I *do not believe* that this solution will work' would be briefly rehearsed putting emphasis where the italics are. Then, adjust the words to 'I *do believe* that this solution will work'. Rehearse again (now more thoroughly) trying to recreate the same voice and body language you used on your first rehearsal.

What if my message is nothing but bad news for the audience?

Let's start with the obvious – don't smile, be serious and adopt a relatively formal approach. Do not say anything like 'I know how you feel about all this' because the audience may well think this is patronising as you couldn't possibly know how they feel. Typically, such presentations attract multiple questions and you should allow more than enough time for them, if not an opportunity for them to ask questions as they think of them over the coming days. I would suggest veering towards a relatively brief presentation, protracting it will cause more unsettlement and potentially anger amongst the audience.

What if I ask for questions and there are none?

You could ask yourself a question to get things started using the likely questions you had pre-prepared to answer, but ensure you give some new information in your answer as an incentive to the audience to seek more information. Having said that, if you have silently counted to at least six and nothing is forthcoming, say when you will be available should any questions occur later and close your presentation.

What if I panic or get flustered at question-time?

The chapter on nerves should help, but if you suspect that this might happen, you will probably feel more comfortable if you sit down (staying in the sight-line of every member of the audience). You could have a blank pad of paper to write down the questions as they are asked during which time, answers will often occur. You can also pre-arrange to bring additional people (resident experts) onto your stage to help answer some of the questions.

What if no-one participates? In my last presentation, everyone just sat there looking at me and wouldn't say a word...

Firstly, it may be that no-one joins in because they are confused as to what you want them to do – ask yourself whether or not you might have delivered a confusing message and try again. Ask for any questions about what you are asking them to do and silently count to 10 – usually this will prompt them to act or speak. It can be intimidating if you have asked individuals to work on their own (they could have a fear of failure), so you could change the format (but not your request) to form small groups to move things along. Step back from the centre of the stage and stay silent. Visit each group and talk through any concerns that they might have. During this time, be careful of your tone and body language – it may be prone to signal your frustration or displeasure.

What if my last presentation was just one big disaster?

I would strongly disagree with the question! Every presentation has its good points. Every piece of feedback and every time you see another person presenting is an opportunity to learn. You can learn from presenters that inspire, from those that bore and you can learn from your own experience. So learn from it and, as the expression goes, if you fall off a bike, the best thing to do is to get straight back on.

If I should only aim for one goal when presenting, what should it be?

To enjoy giving presentations.

Index